Lines from a
Mined Mind

Lines from a
Mined Mind

The Words of
John Trudell

Foreword by Louise Erdrich

FULCRUM
GOLDEN, COLORADO

Library of Congress Cataloging-in-Publication Data

Trudell, John.

  Lines from a mined mind / John Trudell ; foreword by Louise Erdrich.

     p. cm.

  ISBN 978-1-55591-678-7 (pbk.)

  I. Title.

  PS3570.R758L56 2008

  811'.54--dc22

                                    2008003466

Printed in the United States of America

0 9 8 7 6 5 4 3

Designed by Jack Lenzo

Fulcrum Publishing

4690 Table Mountain Drive, Suite 100

Golden, Colorado 80403

800-992-2908 • 303-277-1623

www.fulcrumbooks.com

Contents

Foreword

Now that you have this book by John Trudell in your hands, please let go of anything that might come between you and the words. Let go of other people's poetry and music, and let John define both. Let go of who you think you are and what you do in life and any sort of politics. Let go of belief; let go of disbelief. Let go of expectations that imprison your experience. Let yourself be part of what follows your letting go— ride the steep crest of your acceptance. Just be here.

Your mind is also mined by your perceptions and by what Trudell calls the Great Programming. It is difficult to let go of what is so knitted into the fabric of our thinking. If you have to stand on your head for a while before you start reading, then by all means, begin now.

When John comes to visit and talk or read poetry at Birchbark Books, I always undergo a gentle wave of shock halfway along. I realize that I am in the presence of a being who has dropped the postures of ego and destroyed the social filters that keep us at a safe distance.

So lose your filter. It is really the only way to let these lines touch you.

Louise Erdrich

Introduction
From Somewhere inside My Head

The reality of being   Being just is
We are being being human being
Our human is temporary
An experience of being
In the evolution of being

As human beings
Our relationship to the reality of power
Is in our being being human being
In our human form our DNA bone flesh blood
Is made up of the metals minerals and liquids
Of the earth   We are forms of the earth
All things and forms of the earth   Are made
Of the same metals minerals and liquids
Earth is the mother   All our relations

The being part of human and all other forms
Is in our relationship to sun sky universe
Sunlight is the seed bringing life to
The water-bearing womb that is Mother Earth
Life is a form of the energy of being
All forms of the earth have being
Our power in being is in spirit energy essence
We manifest our power through our human
All things and forms of the earth have
The same relationship to sun sky universe
Father Sky Mother Earth   All our relations

As human beings we currently live in an industrial
Tech no logic programmed perception of reality
We know they (the industrial civilizers—the miners)
Can take the bone flesh and blood of the earth
Called uranium and fossil fuels out of the earth
And put it through a mining refinement process
And convert its being into a form of energy for fuel
This energy is used to feed the machine
This mining refinement process produces toxic and
Other poisons at all levels of manufacture and uses
These toxics and poisons are left to feed on the living

In our human form in this industrial tech no logic
Programmed perceptional reality   The miners mine
The being part of human being by programming our
    intelligence
Converting our being into a form of energyfuel used
    to run
The authoritarian obedience is freedom   violence and
    excess
Are deified   rationalized justified religious salvation
Pretense versus reality industrial predator class
    civilization

Industrial tech no logic civilization is the mining
    process
The intelligence of each arriving human generation
Is programmed to perceive the reality that meets the
    needs
Of the industrial society each human generation
    arrives in
The human beings are individually and collectively
    mined

This mining process also leaves behind poison and
toxic waste
These poisons and toxics are the fears doubts and
insecurity
That affect the human beings' perceptional reality in
such a way
The human becomes separated from the being at the
expense of being
Resulting in human beings viewing life through their
fears and inabilities
Further compounded by hiding behind masks of
pride and progress
The mining process appears to have the effect of
diminishing the
Memory of being   of being human being   no longer
recognizing
Ourselves replacing our identities with the industrial
identities
Of citizen class gender race age religion victim and
whatever

How many industrial human beings have the
experience
Of feeling powerless and while having this experience
How bad can we make ourselves feel and how does
this
Feeling affect the other human beings we interact
with
The extremes these negative feelings can be taken to
Reflect the depths of the power of our intelligence
unleashed
As we incoherently and chaotically react to the
programming
Separated from any understanding that these
intensities are power

Ironically we find ourselves in a dimensional reality
        where we feel
Powerless to deal with the various situations we find
        ourselves in

That same power of our intelligence used coherently
        creates
Our ability to generate our energy in ways that are
        healthier
To the well-being of the earth and the evolution of
        human beings
As human beings how we use our intelligence to
        perceive reality
Dictates how we will use the power of our intelligence
As human beings it is time to take responsibility for
        the power of our
Intelligence and use the power of our intelligence to
        think coherently
This isn't about whether we can or we can't
This is about whether we will or we won't

The miners are mining our human being as a way of
        eating our spirit
These lines from a mined mind could be about spirit
        making an escape
Or these lines could just be some of the crazy falling
        out of my head

Tribal Voice

1983

When today feels like yesterday's leftovers
and tomorrow's going to be more of the same
kinda like dodging the bullet again and again
time crawls because it knows what's coming

Listening:
Listening
One Time
Grandmother Moon
Grandfathers Whispering

Voices Catching Up:
Last Rush in Babylon
Arms Race
Alone

Heart Taker:
Brown Earth Color Woman
Heart Taker
The First Time
Sheltered Moments

Living in Reality:
Sung in the End
Endure
Living in Reality
Diablo Canyon
It Took the Times
For Ronald America
Industrial Slave
Without Earth

Listening

I was listening
To the voices of life
Chanting in unison
Carry on the struggle
The generations
Surge together
In resistance
To meet
The reality of power

Mother Earth
Embraces her children
In natural beauty
To last beyond
Oppressors brutality
As the butterfly floats into life
We are the spirit of natural life
Which is forever

The power of understanding
Real connections to spirit
Is meaning our resistance
Our struggle
Is not sacrifice lost
It is
Natural energy properly used

One Time

I was visiting with my relatives
The clouds the mountains
The sky the trees
My relatives touched my spirit

Nudged it lovingly
Listen to us impatient one
We are forever

You must remember the gentleness of time
You are struggling to be who you are
You say you want to learn the old ways
Struggling to learn when all you must do
Is remember   remember the people
Remember sky and earth
Remember the people
Have always struggled to live
In harmony in peace
Struggle against selfishness and weakness
So the people may live as nations

The old ways are hard
The people have always had
To work together
Remember impatient one
Remember and live
Do not be afraid of truth
Respect discipline
Share your life
So the people may live

Honor sky and earth
Honor yourself
Honor your relations
Remember impatient one
The gentleness of time

Grandmother Moon

You are more than light in the night
You are more than the moon
You are spirit connection
Your energy is our life
You are memories to generations past
You are the creator of sensations
That will always last
You are the knowledge the teacher
The influence to keep the people sane
You are a healer for spirit pain

Grandmother moon
We love you and we are angry
At the invaders who trash you
And violate our universe with
Their mechanical uncleanliness

We pray for you for us and for the
Invader who just can't comprehend
Respect love or the balance of life
We do not join the invading madness
From the way they act
It speaks of spirit sadness
Machine money progress
Is the cause of our common abuse

We see you grandmother
We feel you
We love you
We know through your reality
We will endure
We are one
We pray for you
We pray to you

Grandfathers Whispering

Grandfathers whispering
In the wind
Rejoice at the life
You are a part of
Natural energy
Bound to natural laws
You will survive this
Temporary madness imposed upon you
Natural life is longer
Than oppressors illusionary insanity
Spirits experience human deeds
But need not end
This is just one place of changes

Spirit life is forever if you want
The universe is your home
You can survive here
Do not let them kill you
Keep your spirit strong
For distant stars and distant drums
Are the memories of spirit infancy
Children of earth let the spirit live
So you can grow in your place
                              In the universe

Last Rush in Babylon

Last rush in Babylon
Voices catching up voices catching up
Watch out child watch out child
Babylon falling down falling down

Society a broken promise
Economies war citizen whores
Political pimps
Leaving us flat on our backs
Trading today
Waiting for the promised land

Roles playing roles
Covering every days fear
Going off to work
Having the job done on us
In the eyes of god
Building the bomb
Loving thyself hating thyself
In the illusion

Voices catching up voices catching up
Watch out child watch out child
Babylon falling down falling down

Caligula laughs loudly through time
Twisting love to get at the sexes
Class is material consumed
Designer worlds create electric impulses
Turning down life the real good-bye
See it in our face see it every place

Last rush in Babylon
Voices catching up voices catching up
Watch out child watch out child
Babylon falling down falling down

Arms Race

Jackboots pounding earth
Military precision
Dissecting elements of life
Taking apart instead of healing
Generals and gods
Fascists and oil wells
Man images and machines
Petrochemical societies
Trying to hide the sun

Jackboots pounding earth
Creaking leather boots
Dead cows crying
In a world turned
To a planetary slaughterhouse

Wandering amongst the opulence
Wondering what not to touch
Times not knowing times getting bit
Times of temptation times of seduction
Wandering in the poverty touched by everything
Knowing the bite no time for temptation
Only time for doing

Babylon in terror
World run over by machines
The economics of captured dreams
The rich are the poorer
While the poor are waiting

Everyone pretending to live
Calling exploitation progress
Calling submission freedom
Calling madness profit
Calling earth a plan et
Plaguing her with civilization

Alone

We see you in your loneliness
Sometimes we wonder
Which is lonelier
Being alone together
Or being lonely
Alone

With no protection that you know of
Principles replaced by nothing
The lies becoming desperation
Outrageous violence
Internal and external

Forming distractions from life
Making the loneliness
A new type of alone
Alone with your machines
Alone with your fear
Alone with your oppressor
Alone with roles played
Alone from the past
Alone from the future

Stranded in the universe
Separated from earth sun moon sky
With only god to comfort you
While he sanctions war and greed

Messengers clubbing you
Heavenly threats and promises
A basis for exploitation of everything
Even yourself

Giving up together
Surrendering
Alone

Brown Earth Color Woman

Brown earth color woman
Takes me into the secrets of her sighs
When I step into the brown of her eyes
I find sight of special dreams
Fluttering eyelashes and fluttering hearts
Dancing in magic no one understands

When I step into the brown of her eyes
I find the comfort of a friend
A friend sharing shelter
When only a friend can know too

When I step into the brown of her eyes
She teaches loving through caring
Snuggling softly in my heart
Helping me to just feel good

When I step into the brown of her eyes
The mysteries are different from confusion
Illusions are handled by seeing through
Clearly there is life ahead

When I step into the brown of her eyes
Brown earth color woman
Takes me into the secrets of her sighs
Gentling me in a balance of passion

Heart Taker

Smiling into
Eyes hungry for smiles
You take me where I want to be
You're my heart taker
You're a brand new day
Bringing me in view of the sun

I see the sun rise in your laughter
I hear the forever songs in your kiss
I feel the future in your beating heart
I abandon loneliness for your embrace

You're my heart taker
Come to take my heart
Before it fades away
Blending into my dreams
Showing me secrets of life
Holding my hand in the universe
You put together a breaking soul

Smiling into eyes hungry for smiles
Enchanting today with your magic
Tomorrow can't help but be good
You brought the world back to me
When I thought I wanted to drift away

You're my heart taker
Taking me to joy
Gentling me during a life storm
Lifting me
Between the clouds and the sky
Bringing me in view of the sun

The First Time

The first time
Your eyes caressed mine
To say it was like magic is to tame
The gentle passion and moments
Shared in the seeing of a glance

You took my hand
And opened my heart
To the beauty
Of what I did not see
I tried to understand
Why and how
These things happen
But you explained so much
With your laughing eyes
To make me
Not waste my time worrying
Or wondering is this meant to be

The first time
Your eyes caressed mine
The winds sang their songs
The sunshine shivered with joy
Warming the life within me

Sheltered Moments

Tender love in sheltered moments
Blowing my mind from the beginning
I was drifting through trying
Trying to live a life

Good things happening suddenly
When the days were dark
You brought the sunlight nights
Touching me in your being
Tender love in sheltered moments

You were fame you were fortune
You were peace you were vision
Things I thought I wanted and
Things I really needed
Blowing my mind from the beginning

Your kiss melted the night
Beauty burned in forever fires
Heartbreak heart beating wildly
Flaming love sparks and stars
Showering the world

Tomorrow is today is yesterday
In your kiss time didn't have a chance
Tender love in sheltered moments
Blowing my mind from the beginning

I was drifting through trying
Trying to live a life

Sung in the End

The children laugh
The old ones laugh
The newborn cry
The elders weep

The knowledge of
Infants and elders
Separated only by years

Adulthood lost
To grown-up fear
The only security
Being insecurity
Changing crying
To weeping

The wisdom of
Infants and elders

Crying and laughing
Weeping and laughing
Songs in the beginning
Sung in the end

Endure

The people cry out
Tears of anger
Tears of sorrow
Flowing
Giving birth to resistance
Young ones
To remember struggle

For the people cry out
Tears of happiness
Tears of joy
Washing the pain
Cleaning the spirit
Giving strength

The generations
Remembering the past
To rebuild the future
For weeping is
Another way of laughing
And resisting and
Outlasting the enemy

Living in Reality

Calling us red Indians
We have been the colors
On a chameleons back
Changing with time
Altering the larger pattern
Surviving genocide
Because we have to

Living in reality
We are targets of your unfairness
With warriors for targets
You create your own destruction
This is how we bring you down
Target by target you wound yourself
Using your greed we watch
Your spirit fade

Living in reality
We can endure your cages
Your bullets your lies
Your confusion
We know you have
Destroyed your peace

Living in reality

You only exist

Diablo Canyon

Today I challenged the nukes
The soldiers of the state
Placed me in captivity
Or so they thought
They bound my wrists in their
Plastic handcuffs
Surrounding me with their
Plastic minds and faces

They ridiculed me
But I could see through
To the ridicule they brought
On themselves
They told me squat over there
By the trash
They left a soldier to guard me
I was the Vietcong
I was Crazy Horse

Little did they understand
Squatting down in the earth
They placed me with my power
My power to laugh
Laugh at their righteous wrong
Their sneers and their taunts
Gave me clarity
To see their powerlessness

It was in the way they dressed
And in the way they acted
They viewed me as an enemy
A threat to their rationalizations
I felt pity for them
Knowing they will never be free

I was their captive
But my heart was racing
Through the generations
The memories of eternity

I was beyond their reach
I would be brought to the
Internment camp
To share my time with allies

The last time I saw them
They were standing
In their twelve hour shifts
Addicted
To their chain of command
Waiting to be told what to do
Forgetting about me
Thinking
I was just another protester
They were finished with

Never understanding
I am not finished with them
For I am the resistance
And as always I will return

It Took the Times

It took the times
We didn't care
About living
To learn
Survivors survive
Whether they
Want or not

It took the pain the grief
And the dying
To remember
What gets forgotten
In the living
It took the lessons
Of a thousand generations
To get through the
Time of yesterday

It took the joyful songs
Of laughter to last
Beyond today
Into tomorrow

It took the fragrance
Of a womans touch
To realize
Brothers and sisters
Are never alone

It took the joining
Of earth and sky
To create
Centering the universe

For Ronald America

This time I almost wanted to believe you
When you said it would be all right
You wanted to end the suffering
And the deliberateness of the wrongs
Were only in my imagination

This time I almost wanted to believe you
When you implied the times of
Sorrow were buried in the past
Never would we have to worry
About shadows and memories
Clinging and draining the strength
From our souls

This time I almost wanted to believe you
When you spoke of peace and love and
Caring and duty and god and destiny
But somehow the death in your eyes and
Your bombs and your taxes and your
Greed and your face-lift told me

This time I cannot afford to believe you

Industrial Slave

Industrial slave
Capitalist and Communist
Imperialist
Smiling with false faces
Beckoning us
With their lies about progress
Wanting us to enjoy
The rape of earth
And our minds

Industrial slave
Forked-tongue
Legalistic contract chains
Turning our visions
To technologic nightmares
National security warmakers
Desecrating the natural world
And gods still trying to get over
What you done to his boy

Industrial slave
Material bound
Law and order
Religious salvation
Individually alone

Industrial slave

Without Earth

Without earth
There is no heaven
Streets of gold
Angels wings eternal life
Corporate reich nuclear regimes
Maximizing profit eating identities
Plundering natural allies
As though earth is dead

Allowing religious rite
Collection plate tributes
To church and state
With Christ still hanging
From the cross
Echoing industrial war cries
Warring against body and soul
Attacking spirit
Lying to enslave with an illusion
About freedom

Without earth there is no heaven
Earth and sky universal power
Life energies creative flow
In which we are a pattern
To keep balance
Harmony a gift
An appreciation to enjoy

Honor life
Without earth
There is no heaven

Little Daughter

Little daughter
You are so small
For a big woman
So soft for someone
Who must be so strong

Little daughter
I hold you in my arms
I laugh and am happy
At your baby girl smile
To say I feel good
Is not enough

Little daughter I walk with you
Through the dimension called time
For what are minutes days or years
Compared to father daughter
Places in eternity

Little daughter
You the delicate infant child
Carry the innocent reality
I pray for your protection
Prayers to help you through
This life experience

Little daughter the times I hold
You next to me I am flowing
An infinity of love to fill the times
I cannot hold you next to me

Little daughter
I am always with you
Even when
You cannot see me there

Sister, Sister

Sister, sister
I want to talk to the woman in you
We're under siege in a troubled time
Sister, sister won't you hear my voice
I'm your brother but I've made the mistakes
Of a man   sometimes it's lonely being a man
The programming has its affect
Isolation is such a cruel thing

Sister, sister
Won't you understand
They took your brothers
Turned them into men
Like they took our sisters
Turned them into women

Sister, sister
We are all the family of earth
They have taken us away
In their new clear war
Taught us to compete and abuse
And blame each other
While we're all being used

Sister, sister hear my heart
It's time to bring the family back
Together we must remember earth
We must remember what life is all about

Sister, sister I am your brother
Every time I've ever hurt you
I've always hurt myself
Sister, sister hear my voice
It's all up to us
We have a choice

Tears of Salt

Crystal clear tears of salt
Come when my heart
Talks with sadness
The tears flow
My emotional rivers
It's no damn use to pretend
Pain will not rise again

Crystal clear tears of salt
Help my heart
To feel for something
When I do not want to
Clear my vision
See my peace
Men don't cry
Indians are stoic
I tell that to my heart
To my eyes
They just laugh at me
And sometimes
When my spirit hurts
They make me cry

Crystal clear tears of salt
Purify my memory
Help me understand
This is not the beginning
Nor the end

For My Children

To the people I can talk
When it comes to you
I know what to say
It's I just don't know how

I love you
That's not a question
Showing it has been confusing
My life has drifted all ways
Somehow I could just never stay
I've rationalized
I'm headed to a goal
Yet sometimes
My heart hears me running
To a future always from the past

I love you
Don't want you hurt
I want you to realize your potential
I've always been afraid to interfere
My bias my prejudice my doubt
The weaker sides of me

I had to protect you
Make you stronger
Compassion is to be
Your companion
As you head to your destiny

I've tried the only way I knew
Please try to understand
I didn't know what else to do
And
I love you

Yesterdays Laughter

Yesterdays laughter
Is the balance for today
Todays tears
Are the cleansing
For tomorrow

We started out so long ago
There was no one to teach us
What we had to know
The days were ours
The times they were extreme
We did our best and
We did our worst in
The constant struggle
To understand why

Illusions and fantasies
Battering us
Teaching us the hard way
Forcing us
To find a right way
Shelter and comfort
Coming where we found it
Constantly moving
It was like being chased
By something we did not
Understand

Many are the times we could
Have just laid down and died
But the will of life
Helped us to survive
As we travel through life
With yesterdays laughter
The balance for today
And todays tears
A cleansing for tomorrow

Young Ones Listen

Young ones listen
Remember who we are
Remember where we are
Do not take the word of America

Listen to them as in caution
Live among them as in surrounded
Live not as they live
Live to appreciate

Seconds ago in eternity
Ancient ones decided
Way before wounded spirits
Dreams shattering under aggression

Earth is mother we are children
The protection is our innocence
Seconds ago it was decided
We are the middle of forever

Look for your medicine
There is a white world gone mad
Thinking protection is in force
Greed the machine preys on them
But they will not admit it
Or do anything about it

They have no medicine
With backs turned
On children and elders
They do not even care for
Air or water or land or life

Too confused to care
Is no way to live
Young ones listen
Remember who you are
Remember where you are
Remember why you are

Trying to Forget

Trying to forget   the hardest part
Of trying to forget   is the
Remembering forgetting brings back
I thought you were like
The things that have happened
Things and thoughts I'd put away
But you are you more than
Can just be put away
How frivolous of me
To assume I could regard you
As a thing or a thought

Trying to forget only makes me remember
Emotions we share in our spirit hearts
The delights and the anger so vital
Our wildness making us quick to burn
Bridges behind us and ahead of us
Changing compromise to submit
Looking for happiness finding regret

Sometimes you appear
It's in a song a phrase
Sometimes it's a laugh
Sometimes it's a vision
Of you near to me or
A remembrance of a touch
A kiss or some silly thought
We shared

Times are I wonder what went wrong
Maybe our impatience stopped us
From taking the time to learn
What we thought we already knew
Trying to forget
Only makes me remember you

When You Left

When you left
I knew you had to go
Water came into my eyes
I cried then I laughed
Because
Sometimes I just don't know
I wanted you to stay but you
Weren't really here anyway

Or if you were
It was for just a while

I've run it through my mind
And rerun it through my heart
I loved you more
Than I could say or
Show
Like I say I loved you more
But that's something
Only I could know

Water came into my eyes
I cried then I laughed   what's
The difference anyway
Laughing and crying
The tears taste just the same
I held you but I didn't hold you
And in the end I guess
I only kept myself

Her Beauty

Her beauty is like a dancer in the night
Carrying rhythms others can only imagine
Everyone wanted her yet no one kept her
Beyond a fleeting moment when all seemed right

She left on her own
Driven away by what they had
To keep to themselves   he was one of those
Thinking to claim what others took long ago

They could never share the secrets
For their secrets are shames mistakes
Kept quietly making noise
Only when crashing down
Upon them like invisible walls
Not able to stand on their own when
They sold beauty for things
Their hearts never understood

Pretending
What others could not see
Was connected to reality
They made it easy to believe
But almost impossible to live together
They traded depth for surfaces
Trading until they traded it all away
For misunderstandings

Her beauty
Is like a dancer in the night
Carrying rhythms
Others can only imagine
Everyone wanted her
Yet no one kept her
Beyond a fleeting moment
When all seemed right

I Went So Willingly

I went so willingly
Thinking about knowing
The beauty of your face
Your smile your charm
Dazzle
These sometime broken eyes

Your spoken thoughts
Of love and laughter
Placed the chains
Around me so tightly
I didn't know at first

I went so willingly thinking about
Knowing the beauty of your face
Things went wrong they often do
You grew to need me less
I went into needing you more

One day seeing we were both in a
Pretty prison
All I could do was escape
I went so willingly thinking about
Knowing the beauty of your face

Like a Butterfly

Like a butterfly
With a fading heart
She needed someone
To care for her
When she couldn't find it
She ran back
To the mistakes

Anger
An uncomfortably
Comfortable emotion
Greedily spread
Over those who love her
Safer than taking a chance

What we try to hide
We never can
Beyond placing it
In ourselves
Wounds
Voluntarily inflicted
Creating our own betrayal

Worrying
About being used
As we use up our time
Scaring away the balance

Mental M-16s
Mowing down the enemy
Insecurity
Turning trust into targets
In a battle we don't understand
With industrial greed the victor

Like a butterfly with a fading heart
She needed someone to care for her

All That Was Left

All that was left
Were the pictures she took
Capturing the past in a prison
Not unlike the one
They locked themselves in

She said good-bye the other day
Loving him was lonely
Lonely as she'd ever been
Her life was standing in a space
Where laughter was a disguise she wore
As a shield to protect the world

She said good-bye the other day
Her feelings couldn't be helped
It wasn't anything he'd done
It was just that the prisons
Building around her
Separated even him from knowing
Laughter was a disguise she wore

She said good-bye the other day
She felt out of place
Looking for a place
Her American dream
Hadn't prepared her for this
She felt programmed somehow
She had to find the way to where
Laughter is real
And disguises aren't necessary

All that was left
Were the pictures she took

The Ones Who Knew Me

I would like to thank you
For putting up with
What I never could
It seems the extremes
Were more than I could bear

Your patience taught me so much
Too many times I learned too slow
At times the understandings
Were beaten down by insecurity
Your acceptance of me
Really was something
The times I hurt myself
Bringing it all down on you
You reached out
With love and tolerance

You were always there
When I needed
You steadied me gently
Carrying me
Into each new day
Changing names
Changing faces
Supporting me
Keeping me going

Never Too Loudly

At times they were kind
They were polite
In their sophistication
Smiling but never too loudly

Acting in civilized manner
An illusion of gentleness
Always fighting to get their way

While the people see
The people know
The people wait
The people say
The closing of your doors
Will never shut us out
The closing of your doors
Can only shut you in

We know the predator
We see them feed on us
We are aware
To starve the beast
Is our destiny

The times they were kind
They were polite
But never honest

Very Eyes

We see your technological society
Devour you before your very eyes
We hear your anguished cries
Exalting greed through progress

While you seek material advances
The sound of flowers dying carry
Messages through the wind trying
To tell you about balance

And your safety
But your minds are chained
To your machines and the strings
Dangling from your puppeteers hands
Turning you twisting you into forms
And confusions beyond your control

Your mind for a job
Your mind for a TV
Your mind for a hair-dryer
Your mind for consumption
With your atom bombs
Your material bombs
Your drug bombs
Your racial bombs
Your class bombs
Your sexist bombs
Your ageist bombs
Devastating your natural shelters
Making you homeless on earth
Chasing you into illusions fooling you
Making you pretend you can run away
From the ravishing of your spirit

While the sound of flowers dying
Carry messages through the wind
Trying to tell you
About balance and your safety

A Dimension Called Loneliness

Trying to isolate us
In a dimension called loneliness
Leading us into the trap
Believe in their power
But not in ourselves
Piling us with guilt
Always taking the blame
Greed chasing out the balance

Trying to isolate us
In a dimension called loneliness
Economic deities seizing power
Through illusions created
Armies are justified
Class systems are democracy
God listens to warmongers prayers

Tyranny is here divide and conquer
Trying to isolate us
In a dimension called loneliness
Greed a parent
Insecurity the happiness companion
Genocide conceived in sophistication
Tech no logic material civilization
A rationalization
Replacing a way to live

Trying to isolate us
In a dimension called loneliness

To God

We hope you don't mind   but we would
Like to talk to you   there are some
Things we need to straighten out   it's
About these Christians   they claim to
Be from your nation   but man you
Should see the things they do   all the
Time blaming it on you

Manifest Destiny genocide   maximized
Profit sterilization raping the
Earth   lying   taking more than they
Need in all the forms of the greed
We ask them why they say it's gods
Will   damn god   they make it so hard
Remember Jesus   would you send him
Back to them   tell them not to kill
Him   rather they should listen
Stop abusing his name and yours

We do not mean to be disrespectful
But you know how it is   our people
Have their own ways   we never even
Heard of you until not long ago   your
Representatives spoke magnificent things
Of you which we were willing to believe
But from the way they acted
We know you and we were being deceived

We do not mean you or your Christian
Children any bad   but you all came to
Take all we had   we have not seen you
But we have heard so much   it is time
For you to decide what life is worth
We already remember

But maybe you forgot

Look at Us

Look at us
We are of earth and water
Look at them
It is the same
Look at us
We are suffering all these years
Look at them
They are connected
Look at us
We are in pain
Look at them
Surprised at our anger
Look at us
We are struggling to survive
Look at them
Expecting sorrow be benign

Look at us
We are the ones called pagan
Look at them
On their arrival
Look at us
We are called subversive
Look at them
Descending from name callers
Look at us
We wept sadly in the long dark
Look at them
Hiding in technologic light
Look at us
We buried the generations
Look at them
Inventing the body count
Look at us
We are older than America
Look at them
Chasing a fountain of youth

Look at us we are embracing earth
Look at them
Clutching today
Look at us
We are living in the generations
Look at them
Existing in jobs and debt
Look at us
We have escaped many times
Look at them
They cannot remember

Look at us

We are healing

Look at them

Their medicine is patented

Look at us

We are trying

Look at them

What are they doing

Look at us

We are children of earth

Look at them

Who are they

AKA Graffiti Man

1986

The land of freedom
pay to be born
pay to die
  spend your whole life
    just trying to get by

Richmans War:
Richmans War
Machines for Ancestors
Neon Flash
Thing Is
Lavenders Blues
New Oldman
God Help and Breed You All
Stardreamer Woman
Graffiti Man
He Said She Said
Baby Boom Che
Silent Lightning:
Silent Lightning
Woman Darlin Honey
Shaman (Make a Chant):
Shaman (Make a Chant)
Peace
Bombs over Baghdad
Wildfires

Richmans War

Richmans war industrial streets
Class lines money talks
Turning language to paper pieces
Richmans war free man society
Raging violent insecurity
Nuclear man nuclear woman
Unclear how to act

Richmans war Pershings cruising Europe
America Russia governmental nuclear views
Industrial allies cutting the world
As though they cannot see blood flowing

Richmans war Central America bleeding
Wounds same as Palestine and Harlem
Three Mile Island and El Salvador
Pine Ridge and Belfast

Richmans war the poor
Starving for food
Starving for land
Starving for peace
Starving for real

Richmans war
Attacking human
Attacking being
Attacking earth
Attacking tomorrow

Richmans war
Thinking of always war
Thinking of always war

Machines for Ancestors

With machines for ancestors
New unborn generations
Chemical umbilical cords
Are only wiring
In your electrical progress
Human lives burnt offerings
To the god greed

With lies for ancestors
There is no truth in some futures
Rulers of minds feeding next
Generations souls to the
Control machine
Sacrifice ritual for the
Prophet technology

With isolation for ancestors
There's only the present
Bought by the credit material uses
Forging chains binding you
To destruction
Compliments of your deities
The industrial priests

Neon Flash

No more than neon flash
Trying hiding in eon mask
Have to face who we really are
Some point we have no choice

Distant star distant light
In real world we are human being
In shadow of real world
We are being human

Eon mask for neon flash
Distant thunder distant cloud
Passions reign
Drenched in possession
What we take is hard to do
What we do is hard to take

Some ones are crazy or
Maybe we take turns
Dreaming about some kind of life
We say it could have been different
But it wasn't because we weren't

No matter what it turns out the same
Lot of things we said weren't true
Industrial stories
In an electric instant
Eon mask
Neon flash
Neon flash

Thing Is

Thing is
Nihilistic desires
Civil lies gone insane
Didn't imagine it turning like this

Some things start good and go bad
Some things get bad and stay bad
Are we caught in between
Living a lie or not living at all

Eliminated choices
Lost in dreams we let go
Memories we never got to have
Something else to think about

Waking up in industrial society
Surrounded by angry days
Going through motions of not being
Wanting the best but not expecting it

Surviving paid for in dreams
Feeling like a world alone
Serving god with the devil to pay
Feeling like something in no place

What goes on in hell anyway

Thing is
It has to do with heart
We have to understand
What hearts are for
Before we can get back
To heaven or paradise

Or the power of our mind

Lavenders Blues

He wakes up about noon these days
Vaguely remembering ancient world sunrises
Looking into mirrors where once streams used to be
He shakes his head chasing puffs of sleep from his eyes

What he does must be as real as what he doesn't
Like an electric Indian dueling a video John Wayne
In a place some say is the best country in the world
Reality darts back and forth   night into day
Past to present, day to night, present to future
Exposing a new malaria called material delirium
Neon hits advertising industrial mosquito bites
Hard to find the truth hard to hide the lies
Is paying for the product promoting his demise

His day doesn't even start until dark these days
Old warriors never die they turn to driftwood
Drifting in industrial seas faces on clocks
Confine hands telling lies about time
Imposed illusions who's too restless to rest

The new wilderness   men wolves to be wary of
Wandering promise locked out of childhood houses
What happened to family man once intimately known
Women and love change with changing purpose
Empty arms obvious reminders of empty arms
Unlike so long ago when he had it all together
He tries remembering how he got confused these days
What's accepted as being alright seems too wrong
Trying to survive religions with gods at war
Old ways old habits human dreams struggle on

Fragmentation good with bad hanging between him
Putting him in limbos between dimensions
Living too many days like a lyric with no song
Recognition falters at times but always reemerges
He goes to sleep with the sunrise these days

New Oldman

Tell me mama tell me tell me what I can do
She's got a new oldman new oldman
Tell me mama what can I do
I'm already crying
I'm already falling
I'm already breaking
I'm already dying

Tell me mama tell me tell me what I can do
She's got a new oldman new oldman
Tell me mama tell me tell me
When I see them do I smile
When I see them do I say hello
When I see them do I stop to chat
When I see them do I lie

Tell me mama tell me tell me what I can do
She's got a new oldman a new oldman
Tell me mama tell me tell me
All I remember her charm
All I remember her talk
All I remember her walk
All I remember her love

Tell me mama tell me tell me what I can do
She's got a new oldman a new oldman
Tell me mama tell me tell me
Tell me I'll be alright
Tell me I don't hurt
Tell me I'm not lonely
Tell me then tell my heart

God Help and Breed You All

No I didn't read in his own write
But I read about the Hardy Boys
Looking for the treasure
Spin and Marty didn't find
Turns out it was Annette

Even Indiana Jones didn't figure it out
In the temple of dooms gloom
Rats eyes casting yellow light
On Star Wars in Linda Lovelace's throat
Even Beethoven rolled over for
Johnny be good
While Chuck sat in a prison cell
Listening to Elvis die in the army
Before Sgt. Pepper went into
A strawberry field
And turned into the walrus
Climbing into a bed for peace
In love with a Japanese woman
Hated by an international YMCA
Ex-Jesus freak
Who blew him off the mountain
Martin dreamed about

While the CIA didn't say anything
Hoping no one would imagine
Psychiatric head doctor connections
Or Manchurian candidates
Warmakers   behavior modification
Master plan   killing men of peace
While the queen of diamonds
Reshuffled the deck
Turning up the Ronalds
Reagan and McDonald

In 1985 the wasps were still
Trying to swarm
In radioactive mushroom clouds
Taking space rides with
Charlie's Angels
Into the black hole that was left
After the Hardy Boys found the treasure
And didn't know what to do
So they sold her
For drugs
Bad acid
Bringing to this reality a clarity
Hard to believe
From sea to shining sea

Profits pissing lives into the
Wall Street urinal
Which I don't want to read
But someday I'm going to read
In his own write

God help and breed you all

Stardreamer Woman

Pretty looking good woman
Sweetest heart I'm ever going to see
Won't you share your blanket with me
I don't mean to come on strong or crude
But damn you're a heat wave
Waving me in

When I saw you standing there
In your starshine smile
Heavy vibrations wishing my heart
Feeling good is doing great

World of fire rushing my mind
Lightning flashes in your eyes
Flashing bright flashing on
Won't you share your blanket with me

Stardreamer woman

Stars in the night
Stars in my eyes
Pretty looking good woman
Touching out burning my soul

Put your heartbeat next to mine
Cast your spell wrap us in love
Caring spread like a shield
Eternity grows from an instant

Magic love the bubble won't burst
If you can't stay you need not go
Won't you share your blanket with me
I love you I'm never going to quit

Graffiti Man

Hustling
Hustling down hustling street
Rag man rag woman paper bags full
Street age alerts in tenant childs eyes
Sidewalk playgrounds got to beware
Junkman's in the shadows
Dealing his junk
Beautiful sisters
Deal themselves around
Beautiful brothers
Not so beautiful anymore
So much older than the day before
Ain't everybody tired of being poor

Graffiti man's got something to say
Message in a scrawl message on the wall
Something's wrong not our fault
We gotta be cool our time will come

Open spaces in shopping center walls
Middle-class man middle-class land
Clean enough to be a family affair
Nice place to take wide-eyed child
Controlled climate temperate zones
Neat little shops all laid out
Everything for sale by cash or plastic
Price not negotiable but payment is
Different junkman different junk
Spend some money buy some more

Graffiti man's got something to say
Message in a scrawl message on the wall
Put on blinders dull the senses
Who's worth more than money they spend

Skyscraper building
Corporate corridor
Office suite executive board
High finance big businessman suit
Not stained by sweat or blood
Using money like perfume water
Sophistication smiles
Hide stain and decay
Realistic decisions
In columns and ledgers
Dividing profits among themselves
Spoils of war are spoils of war
Says junkman owner of the junk

Graffiti man's got something to say
Message in a scrawl message on the wall
Down with bosses no more bosses
Something's gotta change
Something's gotta change

He Said She Said

Trust me she said he said
Love me forever he said she said
I can't live without you
I think of you all the time
I want you so much I need you even more
I got to make you mine she said he said
Be mine make me happy he said she said

Their true love burst into flame
Passions a fuel burning higher
How excited they could get
Just thinking of the newness of it all
Every waking hour belonged to the other
Every sleeping hour was the same

Living for now did something to tomorrow
First quarrels fun to kiss and make up
More quarrels turn to fights inflicting hurt
Heated words deadly as napalm
Searing hearts and minds and souls
Hard to forget let alone to forgive
Suddenly there is nothing left
Different flames rage out of control
Changed love to owning nothing to win
The mines gave them something to lose

You lied to me he said she said
You never loved me she said he said
All you ever think of is yourself
I never want to see you again
I hate you he said she said
Get out of my life she said he said

You lied to me you never loved me
All you ever think of is yourself
I never want to see you again
Get out of my life I hate you

Baby Boom Che

You wanna know what happened to Elvis
I'll tell you what happened
I oughta know man I was one of his army
I mean man I was on his side
He made us feel all right
We were the first wave in the
Postwar baby boom
The generation before had just come
Out of the Great Depression and World War II
You know heavy vibes for people to wear
So much heaviness like some kind of
Voiding of the emotions

Their music you know the songs
Life always carries
You know every culture has songs
Well anyway their music was
Restrained emotion
You know like you didn't wanna dance
If you didn't know how
Which says something strange
Well anyway Elvis came along
About ten years after the nuke
When the only generals America had in
The only army she had were Ike and Mac
And stupor hung over the land
A plague where everyone tried to
Materially free themselves
Still too shell-shocked to understand
To feel what was happening

Everything was getting hopeless
Then when Elvis started to rock
The roll just picked up
I mean drabness the beaver showed us
Could only be a foretold future
Who wanted to be Ward and June and
I mean father never did know best
He was still crazy from surviving the war

Like there was this psychotic pall
So widespread as to be assumed normal
Heavy man   you know really
Anyway Elvis showed us an out
You know he showed everyboyman and
Everygirlwoman there's something good
In feeling good
Like a prophet for everyboy everygirl
When someones mom and dad lied
Something about him told us
To be sensual is really okay
Someones mom and dad waltzed us around
Everygirl wasn't supposed to enjoy it
If she did she was bad and everyboy
Well boys will be boys don't feel anything
Take what you can
Marry a decent girl when the fun's done
Like no matter what we did we all were guilty
Maybe someones mom and dad resented
What they missed and while
They were trying to pass it on us
We heard Elvis's song and
For the first time we made up our own mind

The first wave rebelled
I mean we danced even if we didn't know how
I mean Elvis made us move
Instead of standing mute he raised our voice
And when we heard ourselves   something
Was changing you know like for the first time
We made a collective decision about choices

America hurriedly made Pat Boone
A general in the army they wanted us to join
But most of us held fast to Elvis
And the commandants around him
Chuck Berry Buddy Holly Little Richard
Bo Diddley Gene Vincent   you know
Like a different civil war all over again

I mean you take don't be cruel
I want you I need you I love you
And jailhouse rock
Or you take Pat and his white bucks
Singing love letters in the sand
Hell man what's real here
I mean Pat at the beach in his white bucks
His ears getting sunburned told us
Something about old wave delusion
I mean wanting and needing and imprisonment
We all been to those places but what did
White bucks at the beach understand
Other than more straight line dancing
You know what I mean

Anyway man for a while we had a breather
Fresh energy to keep us from falling into the big sleep
Then before long Elvis got assassinated in all the fame
Taking a long time to die   others seized
Control while Elvis rode the needle out
Never understanding what he'd done

It's like we were the baby boom because
Life needed a fresher start
I mean two world wars in a row is
Really crazy man
And Elvis even though he didn't know he said it
He showed it to us anyway and even though
We didn't know we heard it   we heard it anyway

Man like he woke us up
And now they're trying to put us
Back to sleep so we'll see how it goes
Anyway look at the record man
Rock 'n' roll is based on revolution
Going way past 33 1/3
You gotta understand man he was
America's baby boom Che
I oughta know man   I was in his army

Silent Lightning

Silent lightning I saw your face
Silent thunder I heard your name

You are fire I am heat
I am famine you are feast
Look at me looking at you
Oh woman woman woman
What you put me through

You are healing I am wound
I am struggling you are balance
You are singer I am poem
I am darkness you are light
You are laughter I am smile
I am flying you are wings

I am butterfly you are breeze
You are love I am needing
I am reaching you are waiting
Look at me looking at you

Silent lightning I see your face
Silent thunder I hear your name
Oh woman woman woman
What you put me through
Look at me looking at you
Look at me

Woman Darlin Honey

Feel these shivers check this blush
My fast beating heart can only be love
Oh if I could touch you
Then touch you some more
Woman darlin honey
You're the one you're the one

Every smile a really big deal
Got to be you getting me high
You in my head going round and round
Pushing love love give me a fix
I've been down before but I ain't
Down no more
Woman darlin honey
You're the one you're the one

Last night in a dream
Or was it today
You opened my eyes
This fast beating heart
One dream come true
One laugh one sweet talk
One warm breath one hungry kiss
One night can never be enough

Woman darlin honey
You're the one you're the one
Woman you're the one

Shaman (Make a Chant)

Shaman gonna make a chant a chant a chant
Healing in a song a song a song
Shaman gonna make a chant a chant a chant
See who you are you are you are

Shaman gonna make a chant a chant a chant
Listen to your heart your heart your heart
Shaman gonna make a chant a chant a chant
Share love to care to care to care

Shaman gonna make a chant a chant a chant
Natural to be free be free be free
Shaman gonna make a chant a chant a chant
Always do your best your best your best

Shaman gonna make a chant a chant a chant
Kindness a good word good word good word
Shaman gonna make a chant a chant a chant
Open up your mind your mind your mind

Shaman gonna make a chant a chant a chant
Brothers sisters will unite unite unite
Shaman gonna make a chant a chant a chant
Harmony on earth on earth on earth

Shaman gonna make a chant a chant a chant
Shaman gonna make a chant a chant a chant
Peace   no war no war no war
Shaman gonna make a chant

Peace

Peace
Word thought consciousness
Only way to live
Peace
Man woman brother sister
Remember caring love

Peace
People leading kind lives
Leaders aren't leaders people are
Peace
Embrace obligations to truth
Give each generation strong hoops

Peace
Our relations all of life
Harmony in all living things
Peace
Proclamation not enough
Our responsibility   emancipate earth

Peace
Our balance   channel our flow
Determination in human energy
Peace
Past is current to future
We are stronger than we appear

Peace
Warmaker so far out of balance
He can't help but fall
Peace
We come from the beginning
A world with no end
Life

Bombs over Baghdad

Bombs over Baghdad dancers of death
Murder in the air with the next breath
Macho queens selling warmakers toys
Raining destruction good ol' boys

Death bringer in Queen George's eyes
Read his lips warmaker lies
Religious reichs revenging sword
Thou shall kill in the name of the lord

The sheep and the cattle can't keep from milling
Some are more than ready some aren't willing
Volunteering in what they're not dying for
The young republican guard crying for war

Free speech as free as its thought
Controlled behavior reacts as its taught
Fighting for peace can't comprehend
Hate out of love is violent pretend

Vampires drinking blood and oil cocktails
Their violence works it hardly ever fails
When blindman can't see he believes blind
Blind obedience is child of mindless mind

New world order is old world lie
Fighting for peace see how they die
Dragging in god as they turn violent
God says nothing he just remains silent

Stop mad men from running loose
Mother earth woman can't take the abuse
Living right now is living for tomorrow
Time is saying there's no more time to borrow

Vampires drinking blood and oil cocktails
Their violence works   it hardly every fails

Wildfires

I've been the man in love with love
Chasing stars in woman's eyes
Temptation's been my favorite dish
Like a kid dreaming of candy stores
Wanting sweets beyond my reach
Taste of something good calls for more
Been that way since way back when
I've done lots for love except behave

Wildfires burn inside of me
Guess that's the way it's got to be
Rising flame calls my name
Smoke or haze it's all the same
Nature of fire is to burn
Every spark gets its turn

When society looked into my face
Started telling me about my place
I just cringed and stalked away
Work they had in mind didn't appeal
Somehow their rules turned me off
Taking orders from man in charge
Couldn't drink from that cup of tea
Sampling illusions hidden miseries
Heavy chains we can't see
Saw a price I didn't want to pay
Couldn't help but say no way
Only thing to do drift on by

I never meant to do anyone any wrong
And I know I didn't quite pull it off
I never meant to run from responsibilities
Nor waste precious time with apologies
Looking for an out in a world closing in
Trying to be as real as I could be
Confused by definitions of being free
I stepped on some   some stepped on me

Heart Jump Bouquet

1987

In the shadow light
distance waits for the memories
sent to the shadows
for safekeeping

Restless Situations
Listen Closely
Such a Fine Day
Never Never Blues
Heart Chanting
Rockin' the Res
Bringing Back the Time
Heart Jump Bouquet
Poetic Motion
Sweet Things
Tina Smiled

Restless Situations

Reaching for horizons that aren't there
They quarreled again today
Turning her back she feels more like crying
Love turned into contests passion turned unkind
Close to going crazy tempting tempting her mind
Like an ant on an ice cream cone in the sun
Someone knocked down all her sand castles
And she doesn't know why and she doesn't know why

Feelings of her own wandering in restless situations
Want to weep when she faces reality she's in
Want to live want to begin her life again
Feelings of her own wandering in restless situations

Spilling their milk and honey
They quarreled again today
One more quarrel
Their domino theory of quarrels
This man she loved so blind at times
Like two people one she loves one she resents

Dodging in shadows of another's identity
Not stuff young girl dreams are made of
Center stage as woman
One of many still one alone
An actress with all the roles she plays
Trapped somewhere between feelings
Prisoner in love not what she meant
Gilded cages some birds meant to fly
Spaces of walls only walls hear her pleas

Feelings of her own wandering in restless situations
Want to weep when she faces reality she's in
Want to live   want to begin her life again
Feelings of her own wandering in restless situations

Showing a calm face is hard
They quarreled again today
Quarrels line up one by one
Some hang on
Fighting back with words
Words said when hearts tears cry
Why why why
Why's this happening happening
Happening to her

She's not guilty not guilty not guilty
She's a rosebush
Treat her beauty gently
Sweet love her fragrance without thorns
Don't hurt her don't chop her down
She can't live as decoration in a vase
She needs to continue
Continue to bloom continue to bloom

Please lord dear god oh jesus
When when when will things ever change
Damn damn damn it all anyhow
Where she's at
What's she going to do now
Feelings of her own
Wandering in restless situations

Listen Closely

Listen closely
She said it almost a whisper
Her loving eyes smiled into him
Like a feather her lips searched his
Quickly a moment of reassurance

You the one I love no one else will do
Or can do for me what you do
Everything in my life changed
When we met   for the better

It's not what you have
It's what you live who you are
I've been fooled by the haves before
Too many times they have so much
They can't give themselves
Every time I never ended up happy

It's hard for a woman
But we must live our lives
Yes I want to be happy
In that I'm same as everybody
But I'm not everybody I'm myself

I don't know all you've been through
But I know how I feel about you

Feel good about myself
Feel good about tomorrow
Feeling good is important to me
I appreciate it more
Because I've been through feeling bad

So I don't want you to worry
About me and you
I am love with you because I love you
A lover and a friend
What I find in you   you find in me

It's hard for a woman
But we must live our lives
Yes I want to be happy
In that I'm same as everybody
But I'm not everybody I'm myself

Her loving eyes smiled into him
Loving words reaching into his heart
Quickly a moment of reassurance

Such a Fine Day

Such a fine day
Woman in a T-shirt walking down the street
Woman gonna do what a woman gonna do
Woman as a dream looking pretty clean
Woman as a woman got it under control
Straight ahead look she's passing through

Such a fine day
Woman in a T-shirt walking down the street
Sensual rises fabric can't hide
Sensuous movement catchy to the eye
All kind of natural way it should be
Woman of her own not afraid of herself
Woman she is woman she wants to be

Such a fine day
Woman in a T-shirt walking down the street
Man's gonna look can't help himself
Some gonna look in admiration
Some gonna look with desire
Some gonna look and nod their head
Some gonna look pretending they ain't

Such a fine day
Woman in a T-shirt walking down the street
Some women need silks and diamonds
Some women need furs and limos
Some women need to turn cosmetic
Some women have just what they need

Woman in a T-shirt walking walking
Walking down that street
Woman in a T-shirt looking pretty free

Never Never Blues

I never never
Should have turned my head
I never never
Should have believed my eyes
I never never
Should have caught your spell
I never never
Should have rushed too high
I never never
Should have sensed your musk
I never never
Should have painted any dream

Oh girl you're never never never
Gonna make me cry again
If I ever ever ever get through this
If I ever ever ever make it this time
Used up tears never never never
Gonna make me cry no more

I never I never
Should have watched your moves
I never never
Should have wanted your smile
I never never
Should have felt your breath
I never never
Should have tasted your voice
I never never
Should have kept your caress
I never never
Should have wished out loud

Oh girl you're never never never
Gonna make me cry again
If I ever ever ever get through this
If I ever ever ever make it this time
Used up tears never never never
Gonna make me cry no more

I never never
Should have looked more than once
I never never
Should have remembered your name
I never never
Should have thought those thoughts
I never never
Should have saw you not staying

I never never
Should have fell on my heart
I never never
Should have come apart this way

Oh girl you're never never never
Gonna make me cry again
If I ever ever ever get through this
If I ever ever ever make it this time
Used up tears never never never
Gonna make me cry no more

Heart Chanting

Caring love soft love tender love
Heavenly love angel of earth
Girl child all grown up
Beautiful woman sure of yourself
Here I am heart chanting
Boy oh boy man oh man

Give love take love make love
Thoughts I think of you
Floating in a walking dance
You walk you walk your walk
Here I am heart chanting
Boy oh boy man oh man

Instant love wild love hot love
Good things in sweet perspiration
Love and desire running even
Mutual attractions flame to fire
Here I am heart chanting
Boy oh boy man oh man

Strong love love love this love
Reaching from me to you
We must give what we have
What could be can be should be
Here I am heart chanting
Boy oh boy man oh man

Rockin' the Res

Listen to the skies listen to the sound
Something on the land
Something going down
Downpressers speeding by life
Fevers heart burning rivers to cross
Walls of Babylon material noise
Thinking they've touched the moon
Freedom takes a rocket blast
Just another day like yesterday

Rockin' my heart rockin' the res
Woman like you times like this
All that's real connects to you
Happy medicine making me smile
Seeing you laugh getting so near
Rockin' our hearts rockin' the res

Carrying on like he ain't been gone
Warmakers back   back in town
His notion taking care of us
Not same as not even close
Not even close
To our notion of taking care of us
Nowhere to hide nowhere to run
Got no job and prices going up

Warmakers back in town
Just another day like yesterday

Rockin' my heart rockin' the res
No chance we're gonna ever give up
Together we'll dance
Our personal dance
Sweet starts surrendering
Only to each other
These days holding the night
Holding on tight
Rockin' our hearts rockin' the res

Starting wars with the stars and
Working on offing earth
What kind of future is that
Some weird kind of living
Who needs that lie
Pretending we aren't stars too
Really isn't very bright
Earth stars
With jail break in our hearts
Just another day like yesterday

Rockin' my heart rockin' the res
Woman I want woman I need
Times when times do get hard
You sure are some comfort
Rising up love living on carries on
Rockin' our hearts rockin' the res

Rockers hearts rocking res

Bringing Back the Time

You know
I never did get over loving you
This new same old life I'm in
I keep bringing back the time
When I could be still loving you
Your magic gave wings to my heart
Your fragrances were erotic silks
Days nights were canvas for us to paint
Your smiling incantations enchantments

Roaming universes universal love
Caring stronger than hatemakers chains
Beauty protecting truth from lies
I never flew as high as we did again
No more flying as high again
No more touch your face again
No more kiss and make up again
No more scratch your back again
No more is such a long time again
No more no more no more again

Hard finding dreams we left unfinished
None of the reasons are the same
Try closing my eyes looking for focus
Remembering reliving some scenes
You brought me yourself your gift
Showing what you saw I saw it too
Childish laughter running ahead of the rest
Lovebirds falling in and out of the nest
Riding passions winds way lovebirds do
From night we met until night you left

Then like the last good time
You were gone
Only it's hard for me to let you go
This new same old life I'm in
Every day learning about hanging in

No matter how I try to understand
Telling myself about destiny's ways
Pains incognito is this acceptance
There's no way to accept

You know
I never did get over loving you
I keep bringing back the time
When I could still be loving you
I never flew as high as we did again

No more flying as high again
No more touch your face again
No more kiss and make up again
No more scratch your back again
No more is such a long time again
No more no more no more again

Heart Jump Bouquet

Another day of same old same old
Then you walked into the evening
Sparkling energy smiling way you do
When you want to
Talking words mystic rhythms
Round dancing colors in songs
Songs I never heard before
Songs I never imagined before

Like at first sight such a rush
Honey splash cinnamon woman

You shake shake shake me baby
You make make make me lady
Thinking thoughts of stealing fire
Wanting wants wants wanting desire
Wild feeling feeling wild this way
This heart heart jump bouquet

Spectrums circles are hoops
Putting me through changes
Whirlwinds in my head
Imaginations in sultry dreams
Drawing me closer faster
Primal instincts in pursuit
Once sky met wind for first time
It was same with moon and night
Like at first sight such a rush
Honey splash cinnamon woman

No place farther I could go alone
When some falls keep closing in
You'd be a great place to land
Love takes hold with all its might
Nice easy all in the flow
Fragrances loves whispering smoke
Oceans of happy happy enough
High intensity ignition emotions touch
Like at first sight such a rush
Honey splash cinnamon woman
You shake shake shake me baby

Poetic Motion

Every way every day turns
Some say our fates are sealed
Anyway the candle burns
The harvest is the yield

She isn't Barbie but she's had her
Chance at plastic
She isn't hard but she knows the difference
Some streets make
She isn't easy but she's taken a long
Search looking for love
She isn't young but she's not as old as
She feels at times
She isn't old but she never really got
Over being young
She isn't running but she's seen the
Rough in a world too tough

What we see is how we pay
Good thought dreams poetic motion
How we pray is what we play
A loving life needs carings devotion

She isn't afraid but she hears
Mistakes lessons say be careful
She isn't lost but she knows
Confusions frustrations bring
She isn't radical but she can't turn
Away from right and wrong
She isn't mad but she's angry at the way
Everyone's treated mistreated
She isn't unrealistic but she sees this
Shouldn't happen to people's dreams
She isn't surrendering but occasionally
She falls   sometimes by accident

Every way every day turns
Some say our fates are sealed
Anyway the candle burns
The harvest is the yield

Waves of light wait to be found
Good thought dreams poetic motion
Join the circle going around
A loving life needs carings devotion

Sweet Things

When she holds my hand
When she gets real close
Sweet things for my arms
Sweet things on my mind
I call my lady sweetthings

When she smiles her stuff
When she walks that way
Sweet things for my eyes
Sweet things rush my blood
I call my lady sweetthings

When she tilts her head
When she kisses my face
Sweet things looking good
Sweet things just for me
I call my lady sweetthings

When she is tender touch
When she is female fire
Sweet things almost too much
Sweet things never enough
I call my lady sweetthings

When she gives to me
When she takes from me
Sweet things to warm me up
Sweet things I like I love
I call my lady sweetthings

Tina Smiled
(cowritten with Jim Page)

This woman this love
This life we dare to live
This society afraid of what
People might see
Might see through themselves
Or somebody else
Might see what isn't
Meant to be hidden
And somewhere
A wild horse awakens

Last time I saw her Tina smiled
Woman womans love
Hands so gentle eyes so wise
Woman touch I am taken
World so undivided
Where the high wind flies
And somewhere
A wild horse listens

In this world if we're going to live
Some ways we're going to have to stand
Know your heart know your mind
Know how to look know what to find
It doesn't have to be this way
Hanging like a cloud society fear of love
Over our heads shadows in the daylight
And what have they done what have they done
But set it in motion set it in motion
And now it has begun

Times I spent wandering
Back to who we are
Nights we held on
Scattering ourselves
Among the stars
You and me over there
You and me over here

We burned through
To a thousand suns
And somewhere
A wild horse runs

Last time I saw her Tina smiled
Woman womans love
Hands so gentle eyes so wise
Woman touch I am taken
World so undivided
Where the high wind flies
And somewhere
A wild horse listens

Eternity expanding from her hand
Sun rise moon rise grains of sand
Acts of man's violent face
Done in silent night
Won't silence freedom's voice
Here we are reflecting light
Disappearing reappearing
Shadows on the run
And what have they done
What have they done
But set it in motion
Set it in motion
And now it has begun

Tina smiled yeah she smiled
Pretty woman indigo red
Unraveling confusion's heavy thread
Entering and leaving
Tapestries of
Changing worlds
Spirit weaver
Your love has spoken
And somewhere
A wild horse won't be broken

But This Isn't El Salvador

1987

The beast is hungry and calling out names
chaosing the innocent using fear as a chain
in a twisting of the predator and the prey
hunting prey that doesn't know it's the prey

But This Isn't El Salvador

Reading poetry from Central America
After talking with my brother
Suddenly remembering how they kill
Couldn't really say it straight before
They told me you were dead
I died
They told me your mother was dead
I died again
They told me the kids were dead
I died with each name

Fire
The government said accident
They lied
Duck Valley my El Salvador
Our last kiss was our last good-bye
They came for you in winter's night
Winter's wind wailed in mourning
Government people searched for days
Scene of crime digging through ashes
Looking for body parts and disturbing evidence
We buried you all in a large grave
While a blizzard covered us in a blanket of snow
How it stormed terrible pain in the land of the free

Some ones should have noticed
Fewer women laughing
Some ones should have noticed
Fewer children growing up
But this isn't El Salvador

Warm strong willed woman
I still have memories you gave me
Maybe if we recognized peasant eyes
Maybe if we recognized plantation lies
Archbishop Romero would have nothing
On you
Trying not to cry how will I ever stop
Ever see a wounded lion try hiding pain
Watch out it doesn't work
But this isn't El Salvador

At times I feel every embrace we shared
At times every tender moment still lives
Met a Sandinista who touched my cheek
Kind of like you used to
Said to me you are one of us
But this isn't El Salvador

Gentle woman natural mother natural world
Some people won't comprehend what happens
Who wants realities cluttered by acts of war
Have to keep a lot inside at times
Not offending people with words
They don't want to see pictures of
But this isn't El Salvador

Some people told me I'm strong to survive
I'm not strong I'm not weak   no morality
No right no wrong one tear at a time I fall I rise
But this isn't El Salvador

You loved your people
In the face of the American dream
Fry bread and tortillas some wars are the same
Who thinks Wounded Knee and Sand Creek
Happen only in history books   is this not history
We live we die   but this isn't El Salvador

The first look you gave me
Your eyes spoke your spirit your heart
My heart our heart there was no other way
Some ones say we're with you brother
We understand what's been done
Some ones say but this isn't El Salvador
This is America   yes I know
Almost two thousand seasons
We fall we rise   we fall we rise

Born 18

We were born 18
If you think we're strange
You ought to see the others
We were born 18
In the middle of a Babylon dream
It's a crying shame
Is the maim of the game

Learning how to ride out the storm
What did we take what did we steal
What did we keep what did we waste
We wandered with neon eyes among broken lights
Out of sync fantasies unbecoming to reality
Turning over images for others to see

What we can't face looks for us anyway
Breathing down our necks these breaths of fire
We fought the cannibals still nothing's settled
With all these hungers to go around
Master of disguises living double lives
Hiding and smiling we were born 18

Nothing we can do
But conjure what we need
The work going on is the work going on
Is just more pyramids and slaves
Wasting lives to the royal flush
Nothing new happening here nothing new
In the middle of a Babylon dream
It's a crying shame is the maim of the game

We were born 18
If you think we're strange
You ought to see the others

The Newspaper Stand

At the newspaper stand
Walking down a hungry street
Vacant eyes passing citizens by
City boulevards skidding rows
Tucked between storied buildings
Concrete profit erections
Reaching into sky
While policeman's circling blocks

At the newspaper stand
A man sleeps
In a shoe store doorway
Just around the corner
A POW's duty to escape
Bros and a sister riding the needle
While policeman's circling blocks

At the newspaper stand
Somebody needs a dime
For food he says
As yesterday's wine
Falls from his forehead
Someone's brother walks with
Someone's sister
What they do best one of them for sale
While policeman's circling blocks

At the newspaper stand
Newspaper headline warning
Guerilla insurgency Central America
Capitalist must stop Communist plot
Keep world free for democracy
And human rights and human dignity
While policeman's circling blocks

About a Woman

I read an article about a woman
A woman living in the war
In Central America
A woman lost her family
A woman the only survivor
A woman goes to sleep one night

A woman waking up
A woman not a mother anymore anymore
A woman held on she could not scream
A woman not submitting to the enemy
A woman praying for women
On the other side
A woman rebuilding her life
A woman in the Middle East
A woman in Europe
A woman in Africa
A woman in Asia
A woman in North America
A woman in different situations
A woman all the same
A woman pays for man's war

Isn't My Life

This isn't my life I'm living
Trying to fit in where there's no room
Conditioned for roles to play
Keeps changing the shape I'm in

This isn't my life I'm living
Too much mistaking vanity for love
Not sure who I'm fooling
But I don't think it's me anymore
Don't even know
When I changed into a shadow
Don't even know when I lost the battle
Points I tried to prove were too sharp
Running up a score I couldn't handle

This isn't my life I'm living
Trying to fit in where there's no room
Conditioned for roles to play
Keeps changing the shape I'm in
Days wearing away day after day
Accepting what I know I shouldn't
Believing in what I couldn't
Tricking myself with nothing to say
This isn't my life I'm living
A promise isn't as real as I thought
Giving and receiving altered
To sold and bought

The emperor's new clothes aren't my size
Too synthetic wearing truth into lies
Now I understand why the sky is falling
When I hear those long distance sighs
Somewhere my soul keeps calling
Days wearing away day after day
Accepting what I know I shouldn't
Believing in what I couldn't
Tricking myself with nothing to say
This isn't my life I'm living
Somewhere my soul keeps calling

Instant Heat

Something in your look
Straight at me invitation eyes
Fire starting my heart
Instant heat pretty cool

When I saw you
Love woman love shining in my eyes
My leaping heart can't be still
Head over heels falling in love
Love woman love
Drawn to your smile
Too far gone I'm in it now
Feeling good I don't want out
I only want you
Something in your voice
Talking me back
Places I shouldn't be
Let them go come to you
We are ally

Love woman love
You're a prize I've been looking for
Can't remember how long
But I remember you   love woman love
Turning me around turning me on
The search was worth the wait
The treasure is worth the find

Something in your feel
Flesh is flesh soul is soul
Spirit is life
We are man and woman
Way we're supposed to be
Something in our lives
Brings us here
Instant heat pretty cool
Love woman love
You are the one
I am the other one
Together we can fly
Instant heat pretty cool

Thicker Than Blood
(For Billy Joe)

Thicker than blood
Through the hole in the sky
Into seasons of traveling light
Beyond the reason and time of why

I have to smile
Remembering how someone
When they first met us
Once told us one of us was strange
And how after we always laughed
And pointed fingers

Seeing what we saw
Back in those out on the street days
Thinking pain had no end
Souls free spirit being vaporized
Draining humans for pro fit systems
Designer glories for the living dead
Submitting to the lie   ultimate surrender
Mistaken identities cloud futures
With yesterdays broken smiles
Desperate for another chance

But we were wilder than that
We were thicker than blood
Journeys we took
Trying to get away
Watching doors to see
Who's coming back
Passing the judgment passers
While some hid from god
While some searched for god
Very few could feel the light

Thicker than blood
Through the hole in the sky
Into seasons of traveling light
Beyond the reason and time of why

When we all went through too much
You never surrendered no give up
At times we dared not
Speak of what was endured
Back on our feet
When we understood
Warmaker confusing
Torturing the innocent

You never surrendered
During days of show and things to prove
You were rock steady laughing man
Knowing what must be done
You represented what was real
More than rhetoric or illusions grandeur
Like a natural headman from the old days

Thicker than blood
Through the hole in the sky
Into seasons of traveling light
Beyond the reason and time of why

Beauty in a Fade

A man a woman
A sort of love

She was a beautiful woman
But he did a lot of ugly things
To turn her world around
In his own way he loved her too
Trying to be his own man
Conquer the world
When he couldn't
She became his last stand
He was cowboys she was Indians

Some beauty fades
In too many ugly scenes
Glows from flush of love
Turn to flickering hopes
Falling from the clouds
When somebody leans
Today too early
For the future
Too late for the past
What happens to love
The kind that lasts

She wanted what she needed
He needed what he wanted
Being in two worlds existing as one
Confined in the walls of their relationship
Becoming hammers tearing the walls down

Once they shared the same dream
Ends up they both had canvas
Of their own   and their own paint
Then they saw   they only brought
One frame
Her part of the dream alone
Was bigger than that
A man a woman a sort of love

One Side of the Face

One side of the face tells us lies
One side of the face believes those lies
One side of the face believes nothing at all

We were all young together
One throw of the dice
No one left but survivors

One side of the face divided by two
One side of the face a darkening cloud
One side of the face won't stand up

Against the army of the rich
See us watching where they step
Unseeing eyes listening for promises

One side of the face praising love
One side of the face can't hear the praise
One side of the face lost its soul

Changing seasons life gives us age
Who gives us insecurity through the seasons
How many children were unhappy
How many elders grow up lonely

One side of the face has a crooked smile
One side of the face prays for salvation
One side of the face preys with an e

Summers and autumns of our lives
Imaginations trapped
In tech no logic corrals
Industrial hunting grounds
After youth before age   entire lives
Spent   never figuring what happens

One side of the face doesn't know any better
One side of the face is better than that
One side of the face hides from itself
And the other side of the face

                                        Knows it

What Happens

What happens when you're alone
But you're not alone
There are people all around
Heads buried in private sand
Always it comes back
To there's nothing anyone can hear
Words are projectiles
Random firings usually miss the mark

What happens when you know
What you're doing but you don't
Your eyes are dry as dust
While your soul drowns in tears
There's nothing anyone can do
When there's nothing anyone can do

It's your eyes your soul your tears
Your private journey

What happens when you don't know
What happens next
You've seen the scene
So many times already
Waiting for something to go away
Yet there's always something
Unseen velvet walls
Something between you and your self

What happens when you've done
What you were never gonna do again
Another waste the same old story
Spilled wines bitter taste

Holding back your heart
Some type of mistake you keep making
Knowing the weight of your life
Gets heavier not lighter

What happens when you ride it out
But the ride never ends
Always looking for the escape
Forgetting about the chain
Tripping over your own emotions
But never breaking the chain
Paying for every taken chance
Price may be too high to make amends

What happens when you're alone
But you're not alone
What happens when you know
What you're doing but you don't

What happens when you don't know
What happens next
What happens when you've done
What you were never gonna do again
What happens when you ride it out
But the ride never ends
What happens when the inevitability of
Tomorrow arrives
It always does

Things could get better and should
Any day now any day now
This sleepwalking dream
Should step from the shadows
Eventually the sun must burn through
With shining light

At Some Point

At some point there's no point
Always there's a choice
About going through it

Strange ways at dressing the scene
Torn between fighting and caring
Becoming to costumes we're wearing
Some one's worried about looking good
Caught up in what is misunderstood

All dressed up
In the emperor's old clothes
Mirror on the wall
Who's fairest one of all
Seeking respect in threads
Some status heads

A dandelion wanting to be a rose
As old thought dark ages reemerge
Hidden behind the glow on neon light
Alien thoughts dressing civilized
The day burns while the night cries
For someone to remember
Someone to remember

Self-worth thieves stealing through the ages
Ultimate space race star war soup lines
Tribes in flight brother sister gender combat
Mechanical motion spoiling for a fight
All dressed up in the emperor's old clothes
Space race fantasy grooming dark thoughts

At some point there's no point
Always there's a choice
About going through it

Woman Treat

Woman treat woman treat
Pretty style pretty smile
Woman treat woman treat
Mind fragrance flesh
Woman treat woman treat
Walk dance glance

Woman treat woman treat
You got to notice me
Woman treat woman treat
When you smiled into my face
I was gone from wild to tame
Man nothing's gonna be the same

Throbbing heart beating out a song
Love has come to take me
When you smile bluebirds are happy
Winds cuddle clouds

Woman treat woman treat
Notice me hanging from my sleeve
Woman treat woman treat
This isn't make believe
Woman treat woman treat
Can't get you out my mind
Woman treat woman treat
Think I'll think of you

Woman treat woman treat
When you smiled into my face
I was gone from wild to tame
Man nothing's gonna be the same
Singing blood carrying tunes to my soul
Relax lighten up this is the real thing
When you smiled time and space got in the way
There was nothing I could do but thank the day

Woman treat woman treat I'll never get enough
Woman treat woman treat let me be a friend
Woman treat woman treat let me be your lover
Woman treat woman treat let me be with you

Co-Optation

These Indian ears
Hear them supporting
People's revolution
In Central America
And rest of third world
While they tell us our situation
Is different   we must be patient
Their system of laws
Protects freedoms face they believe
But these ears believe different

These Indian eyes
See them struggling along civil
Disobediences cooperation rules
Violent non-violence
Handing human identities
To warmakers national security squads
As if warmaker believes in
Same democracy they do
Pretending civil disobedience by
Cooperating could be
Aiding and abetting enslavement
In these eyes someone's in for
Big surprise

This Indian heart beats
Times they said they understood
As they tried imposing
New missionary positions
Of their love-hate romanticisms on us
Heart beating in a rush we barely escaped
What they said they understood

These Indian dreams
Surround words so carelessly used
As they speak of truth and justice
Their illusions grow like tears
On these dreams as though dreams
Are fires they want put out

This Indian blood flows
As they proclaim freedom
From their point of view
Indian blood flows
Through prison bars
Through business streets
Through revisions history
Through the hole in god's golden halo
Blood flowing back into stolen land

This Indian voice
Carries thoughts
They have no time to hear
Sounds of their industrial power speak
Languages more persuasive to the mood
Protect the environment
But protect the material most
This Indian voice speaks of mother
But who listens

This Indian soul
Lives in and out of their reach
In the wind air water soil sky sun
Moon stars plants animals birds
Memories laughter tears
This Indian past this Indian future
                                    Waits

Song of the Trees

Listen as the trees sing
Their songs
In the wind lyrics and melodies
For the spirit senses

Songs of laughter and life
Timeless things in timeless places
Do not be afraid to be strong
Do not be afraid to love
But always remember

Always remember
Love wisely
The love of being
Free of possession
The love of being
Beyond desire
The love of being
Respect for Mother Earth

Listen as the trees sing
Their songs
In the wind lyrics and melodies
For the spirit senses

Songs of laughter and life
Timeless things in timeless places
Do not be afraid
Remember the medicine is in the time
Live this life to last

Join the time of tomorrow and the past
Be like us serve the creation   we will endure
Listen as the trees sing their songs
Listen   listen

Fables and Other Realities

1991

There are times when laughter is a scream
that can't stand the sounds of screaming
using mask and disguise to muffle the sound
freedoms illusions are the pied pipers songs

Fables and Other Realities
Baby Dolls Blues
Laughing
What He'd Done
Baby What's Happening
Long Silky Caress
The Dream
Teddy Bear Tears
The Needle
Somebodys Kid
Raven
Fire in the Village
Fables (Reprise)

Fables and Other Realities

While the mute proclaimed the glories
Deafman listened closely as he danced
Seeing into pictures blindman painted
Mother Goose and the Brothers Grimm
Laughed knowingly up their sleeves
Grown-ups are the children's children
Captured and taught what to believe
Sampling fables and other realities

Prototype people rigid suit trolls
Near brain dead   under for spacious skies
Gathering storm clouds   rule of law
A falling axe in storm troopers hands
Cruel class deceivers claim god for their side
Making up stories with places for meanings to hide
Dracula drinks deeply while nourishing his trap
The love of mankind an alluring narcotic rap
Sex does love sex is life then sex meant death
Homosexual needles as if laboratories don't exist
Bacterial warfare aids testament to deathmans kiss
Drug master using drugs to blame poverty and crime
Moneymaster cashes in on the peoples golden light
Skulls and crossbones uniformly waiting in time
Raging peace stone satan spoiling for the fight
In wars for souls profits are in casualties
Spilling scenes from fables and other realities

Man woman living behind dark tinted eyes
Concepts of love possess concepts of love
Grown-up fears traveling faster than light
Love is as blind as the people who see
Emotional playgrounds intense as battleground
User words for protection leave a hollow sound
The prince and the maiden don't stand a chance

A fiddler plays but they're too confused to dance
Their love was smooth then the love was rough
The lessons of living didn't teach them enough
There's the man the woman and all those dualities
The material of fables and other realities

Baby Dolls Blues

In a cosmos of temptations leanings
All that went down had many meanings
She saw some light hidden behind the dark
In rivers of loneliness anger left its mark
Many of lifes chapters written by wrong doing men
Gambling to win her desperation not to lose again

A woman holds remnants of girl childs goals
Wandering through dimensions of wandering souls
Much more pain than glory as her story unfolds
The reality is the illusion keeps playing roles
Late night sleeping dreams still coming back
A mind with the blues wearing mourning black

Baby dolls blues a girl now all grown up
The golden chalice turns into a Teflon cup
Playhouse dreams devoured by livings scenes
Everything's something with nothing as it seems

Gnawing pain aching from long time hurt
Suppression memory reflections self-worth
There's a noisy closet behind a locked door
Filled with a past that can't take any more
Searching for the key to let her run free
Life beyond the image see another reality

In love with a man so slow to learn
Standing her ground no more cheeks to turn
Cages were built by what's been done
This sister a prisoner living under the gun
Standing accused she cries that's not me
I'm a real person   why why won't you see

Needing the peace she's searching for
Worn down from those days at war
With private truths she wants to tell
But she doesn't want to be put through hell
When she finds a love that can understand
She'll be free   having found a promised land

Laughing

Laughing laughing laughing begins
Laughing laughing laughing at me
Laughing laughing laughing at you
Laughing laughing crying begins

In burn of fires we started
How quickly I turned into ashes
Your new flame is an old flame
You wouldn't stop loving
The dream split   over again
I'm not sure where I've been
I could have been a horse
When you needed to ride
Escape that darkness
That's your other side
I was holding on to you
You were holding on to him
He was holding on to you

When I looked around
No one was holding on to me
Languages are parts of truths
I trusted your laughter
Right up to the last laugh

Laughing laughing laughing begins
Laughing laughing laughing at me
Laughing laughing laughing at you
Laughing laughing crying begins

A familiar story so I'm told
Someone new was someone old
When my heart couldn't break
My mind could and did
I ran into the memory store
Looking for a happy memory or two
Sorry storekeeper said we don't
Carry those memories here anymore

Guessed I knew what I was doing
Until I paid by coming undone
Too disoriented to feel like a fool
Doesn't love have a golden rule
A familiar story so I'm told
Someone new was someone old

Laughing laughing laughing begins
Laughing laughing laughing at me
Laughing laughing laughing at you
Laughing laughing crying begins

I ran into the memory store
Looking for a happy memory or two
Sorry storekeeper said we don't
Carry those memories here anymore

What He'd Done

First time she heard it hurt the most
Each time she thinks it hurts the worst
Whatever happened to cherish honor
And protect   her dream world
Before her dream was wrecked
First time she heard it hurt the most
Each time she thinks it hurts the worst

When he told her what he'd done
Running around with some other ones
She couldn't believe this turn of luck
Devastation as though she'd been struck
Thunderbolt lighting strike in her skies
Little girl tears in this woman's eyes

She tried finding all those words of expression
How to explain these feelings beyond depression
A true man a true man's love
Is it too much to ask
Her reach for peace on earth
As shattered glass

Trust betrayed
While she saw their love as special
Didn't he know what he'd done
Pulling trigger to this gun
Like a shot through her heart
The pain leaves her stunned
Twisting hard she questioned
Had she done something wrong
Is it really all her fault
She always tried and tried
Girl and woman know realities
Of commitments she made to this man
To this love to this bond to their song

Strange news anger sedates the pain
Then pain sedates the anger
Real news a dream in pieces
Just another empty hole
Picking up pieces
Has an affect on the soul
Each piece
Places its own weight on the mind
Each missing piece
An ocean leaving shore behind

Something chilling
In the world she wants to know
Something to what she didn't want
To already learn   now she knows
You can't turn back the clock
Absorb or deflect
Not to turn into a prison or a lock
Times of caution
She could become a jailer or a key
Check the picture clearly
There's always something to see

Life goes on no matter
No matter what we do what we do
Have to get past these rough waters
She's going through
It's a long long river
And an even longer swim
Reality is in how we swim
Not about how we win

Baby What's Happening

Baby what's happening
In the temple of many scenes
My mind weighs more
Than my heart can carry
Gilded serpent imaginary line
In between the in between
Reality shivered

Baby what's happening
Whatever it was we did too much
Did until we couldn't get enough
Did we find real love
Or were we settling a score
Jade people in jaded love
Found in the house of truth
Shuttering windows with lies

Baby what's happening
Lone wolves can't run with the pack
Lone wolves run with themselves
Human reality multiple duality
Pain splatters on living things
More than once
Too many times to count

Baby what's happening
Painted Jesus cries
Take away this paint
This painting is all painted wrong
The day before day got bad
Footprints raced over feelings
Chasing shadows called the long run
A river is hot like fire on a tear

Baby what's happening
This crazy thread weaves
This crazy thread breathes
In the temple of many scenes
My mind weighs more
Than my heart can carry

Baby what's happening
This crazy thread knows
This crazy thread grows
Gilded serpent imaginary line
In between the in between
Reality shivered

Baby what's happening
In the temple of many scenes
My mind weighs more
Than my heart can carry
Gilded serpent imaginary line
In between the in between
Reality shivered

Long Silky Caress

There's pounding on the door
And a barking dog that won't quit

The lady with the long silky caress
Ran her fingers softly through my heart
An undulating moment shutting down time
Sensual gold rushes coming attractions
Sultry style born in mysteries of the sun
Flame breathes heated sighs gently to the edge
Night turned into one long enchanting rhythm
In the moment of memories all became clear

The lady with the long silky caress
Slow stirring smoking embers of my soul
With heartbeats closing in heart to heart
Bringing what the whirlwind brings
An enchanted forest a waiting nest
Tripping where bursting light bursts
A moment of memories all became clear

Splendor behind closely clenched eyes
Molten rivers blazing trails of thirst
Fast traveling into rains that drench
Gems of love when treasure rules
Emerald fire from the box of jewels

The lady with the long silky caress
Like wild streaking lightning through my veins
Naked juice floating thunders seduction storm
An undulating moment shutting down time
A moment of memories all became clear
A ceremony in the laying of the hands
She gave me shelter with her fire
Whispering I'm your every desire
Do what you must do as you will
I'm the moment for you to fulfill

There's pounding on the door and
A barking dog that won't quit

The Dream

Another day like many other days
She was from her own tribe
The tribe of pretty women
Knowing what only pretty women know
She was from the clan of the birds

It was after dark on the mountain
He followed the sunset to this place
He was from the tribe of the wanderings
Wanderings a wind never let them settle
He was from the clan of many clans

Offering of smoke the dream begins
He told her the story of many stories
The story of many stories was his own
Each story with its own way to go

She said not to worry   he was safe
In the dream   melting in eternal flame
Melting the melting stone   genetic light
Fire flashes from the eternal mind
First fires an intensity that never burns out

The dream engulfed time with all its attachments
Leaving only the ride the ride was traveling light
The other side beckoned in long ago knowing
Purpose of the journey is in learning questions

Allied attractions their list of reasons
There's a purpose always being served
The dream protected them for the dream
Arcing heat warmed their travels
Bringing them back to an understanding
All that was spoken is what was unsaid

Laughter and giving up the fight
Alerted them not to be limited
By perceptions of distorted men
The dream carried them through
The mountain and to another dawn
Another every day

The woman
From her own tribe
From the tribe of pretty women
From the clan of the birds
Smiled accepting the dream
After another dawn
And another every day

The man
From the tribe of the wanderings
From the clan of many clans
Disappeared into the dream
It happened while it never happened
It was only the dream

Teddy Bear Tears

He was a teddy bear
Doing teddy bear time
In a teddy bear prison
For a teddy bear crime

Never meant to go wrong
But the urge was strong
He offed Barbie dolls
'Cause one strung him along
He loved her madly
But she ran around with Ken
He didn't like to lose
His compulsion was to win
It all got out of control
Way rage usually does
He had his pride
She made a fool of who he was

Teddy bear tears
This bear didn't mean to turn bad
Living in a room
With a little girl who had bad dreams
Learning about life and love
Came from the TV screens
Between scenes losing track
Of when madness went mad
Let me be your teddy bear
A memory from his head
Guess it doesn't matter
Because the king is dead

He got carried away
Much more than he meant
He saw her face every place he went
Too many Barbies
Once he started no way to stop
A way of triangles
When you fall from the top

It was all too easy
He kept getting away clean
He ran up a score
To three or four dozen or more
An unexplainable rush
Like a powerful dream
He felt like a bear again
Waging an avengers war

Carelessness tripped him up
In pursuit of the high
Jack in the box surprised his act
No way he could lie
One of the parents busted him

With Barbie hair in his fur
A major mess up was in hanging out
Where the Barbies were
No trial no judge no jury
For his capital offense
No one to hear his side
No way to present a defense
A one-way trip to the garbage can
When justice reacted
The executioner's song
In the morning he'll be compacted

Teddy bear tears
This bear didn't mean to turn bad
Living in a room
With a little girl who had bad dreams
Learning about life and love
Came from the TV screens
Between scenes losing track
Of when madness went mad
Let me be your teddy bear
A memory from his head
Guess it doesn't matter
Because the king is dead

The Needle

I saw my brother in a needle
I saw my brother face the gun
I saw my brother back in laughing times
With every morning a brand new day
With childhood drawn out stretching to now
Until one day every day became the same

I saw my brother in a needle
I saw my brother face the gun
I saw my brother on the run

Living the little time he had
But progress was just too much
More than he really wanted or needed
Society of lies repeated daily by the same faces
Denying balance the lies became truth
What's the difference in dead
And living a lie

I saw my brother in a needle
I saw my brother face the gun
I saw my brother love the wrong ones

Looking for love a long time gone
Alone in relationships
He couldn't communicate sorrow
Felt in each lie told
Finally choosing exile over madness

I saw my brother shooting pain
I saw my brother in a needle
I saw my brother face the gun

I saw my brother

Somebodys Kid

I was crazy before
Now I'm crazy again
I won the fools war
In a game I can't win

Me and bliss playing hit and miss
Me and buzzed forgot where I was
Looking for a disguise that passes
Cutting class in our looking glasses

Sons were acting like their fathers
Mothers acting like their daughters
There was a rich ugly lady who
Thought her money made her pretty

There was a respected powerful man
Being mean with a reckless hand
Told me they were out of civil rights
I looked like a case for sybil rights

Me and Jesús trying to keep loose
Step ahead of the goose-stepping goose
New age world in an old world cage
Supply and demand long on demand
And happiness is in short supply

Dealermans not dealing drugs
Because people do drugs it's so they will
A way of fixing them while they break
As they run out of wishes and hope
He steps in with materials and dope

I was crazy before
Now I'm crazy again
I won the fools war
In a game I can't win

Me and I guess are in a mess
Princess of doublespeak said
Wasn't her doing what she did
I cried don't do me like you done
Can't you see I'm somebodys kid

I was feeling lonesome and blue so
I called my steady maybe up
She changed her number to 976
Guess she's lonesome and blue too

I tried to catch a falling star
When I missed it hit me on the head
What I call falling star struck

Raven

Descending raven in fire of light
Ascending heat from my taken heart
Answering the call of the wild moon
I was there as she called my name

Couldn't help but give my heart away
Raven singing sounds made of night
Recognizing each other from before
Ravens gentle wings spread in flight

First time I've ever had this dream
Good nights ways of quickly passing
Good nights time can be everlasting
Bringing memory back more some more

No feeling of being misplaced
Had this need to be in love
Looking to her eyes I saw my need
Thirsty hunger had to have a taste

No turning back from who we are
We are peoples of ancient star
Spirit helpers in time of need
Descendants of ancestral seed

Chocolate eyes escape in the vanilla village
Fugitives from the vanilla world
I ask her over the line is love a good word
She said yes

Northern lights dance on my mind
Raven a brilliance of the sun
Moisture lasts in worlds we know
We are a river the way rivers flow

Fire in the Village

Fire in the village
The little people can't help but dance
Fire in the village
Dream visions in dreams
Fire in the village
Freedom livings strongest desire
Fire in the village
The little people listen with a fancy step

Fire in the village
A restless drift a wind blowing in
Fire in the village
Smoke in the eyes burning away lies
Fire in the village
A higher kind of love comes of age
Fire in the village
Something good burning away rage
Fire in the village
Look through eyes of the painted face
Fire in the village
Warmaker smothers by his own disgrace
Fire in the village
The little people can't help but dance
Fire in the village
Continuing life flowers are in bloom
Fire in the village
Eternal springs these rivers will run

Fire in the village
An energy storm in gathering light
Fire in the village
Changing night a cloud's going to lift
Fire in the village
Liberty is shining in a new worlds soul
Fire in the village
The little people listen with a fancy step
Fire in the village
The little people can't help but dance
Fire in the village

Fables (Reprise)

While the mute proclaimed the glories
Deaf man listened closely as he danced
Seeing into pictures blind man painted
Mother Goose and the Brothers Grimm
Laughed knowingly up their sleeves

The grown-ups are the children's children
Captured and taught what to believe
Sampling fables and other realities

Fables

Fables and other realities

Reality

Children of Earth

Childs Voice

1992

Programming our intelligence
with the illusion and fantasy of
there's something wrong with us
and enough isn't enough
and too much isn't too much
then turning us loose
on ourselves and the world

Children of Earth
Last Rush in Babylon
See the Woman
Questions
Good Thoughts
One of the Colors
Material Junkies
Some People Say
One Journey
Child of the Dream
Peace with Earth

Children of Earth

We are all children of earth
Kids moms dads aunts uncles
Grandmothers grandfathers
We are all children of earth
The earth is our mother
Mother Earth is for all of us

We must all be kind to our mother
Take care of her and love her
Mother Earth has many children
All living things are her children
The plants animals birds fish insects
Reptiles and the people

The human beings
Have responsibilities
To take care of
The living natural world
The mother takes care of us
Provides all we have
If we do not care for her
She cannot care for us

The human beings have thoughts
And can act on these thoughts
How the human beings think affects
All the living things
Human beings are caretakers
To take care of Mother Earth
Protect her with good thought
We are all children of earth

We are all children of earth
The earth is our mother

Last Rush in Babylon

Last rush in Babylon
Voices catching up voices catching up
Watch out child watch out child
Babylon falling down falling down

Society a broken promise
Economies war citizen whores
Political pimps
Leaving us flat on our backs
Trading today
Waiting for the promised land
Roles playing roles
Covering every days fear
Going off to work
Having the job done on us
In the eyes of god
Building the bomb
Loving thyself hating thyself
In the illusion

Caligula laughs loudly through time
Twisting love to get at the sexes
Class is material consumed
Designer worlds create electric impulses
Turning down life the real good-bye
See it in our face see it every place

The great lie licks its lips
Narcotic concepts
Suffocate the individual
Warmaker and the peace pretenders
In the trance of the vicious circle
Non violence feeds from
Fruits of violence
The great lie licks its lips

Last rush in Babylon
Voices catching up voices catching up
Watch out child watch out child
Babylon falling down falling down

See the Woman

She has a young face an old face
She carries herself well in all ages
She survives all man has done

In some tribes she is free
In some religions she is under man
In some societies she is worth what she consumes

In some nations she is delicate strength
In some states she is told she is weak
In some classes she is property owned

In all instances she is sister to earth
In all conditions she is life bringer
In all life she is our necessity

See the woman eyes
Flowers swaying on scattered hills
Sun dancing calling in the bees

See the woman heart
Lavender butterflies fronting blue sky
Misty rain falling on soft wild roses

See the woman beauty
Lightning streaking dark summer nights
Forest of pines mating with new winter snow

See the woman spirit
Daily serving courage with laughter
Her breath a dream and a prayer

Questions

Do not be afraid
To ask questions
Questions are windows
For your mind
See all you can see
Learn all you can know
The night has answers
As does the light of day

As we are taught
To buy and sell
We must remember
How to give
What to give
A way to live

As we are taught
To own and possess
We must remember
How to love still to care
Why we are here there is a reason
This our world this is our season

Do not be afraid
To ask questions
Questions are windows
For your mind
See all you can see
Learn all you can know
The night has answers
As does the light of day

Good Thoughts

Raven brought beaded serpent
And the Alaskan thunder

Realities yet to come
Good thoughts are good way life
Wrapped in the universe
The unborn sleep in dream time

Day in the sun is on its way
Think good thoughts
Thoughts of lightened mind
Dream dreams dreaming brings
Sense rush of new found find
View where harmonies sing

Follow the sky
Into the blue
You are part sky
Sky is part you

There are stars that bring the night
There are thoughts to bring clear sight
Thinking good makes for strong heart
Nourishment for spirit and soul

A good path a good way to give
Belief creates what we believe
Good words
Good thoughts
Good actions
A way human beings live

Raven brought beaded serpent
And the Alaskan thunder

Follow the sky into the blue
You are part sky sky is part you

One of the Colors

Happiness is how we feel
About ourselves
The good we think
The good we feel
The good we do
We are part of the dream time
Happiness is one of the colors

There are shadow casters
Who trick us about happiness
We are taught to wish for things
To make us happy
We are not taught to dream
For happiness itself

We can't buy happiness
We can't sell it
We can't steal it
We can't borrow it and
We can't capture it but
We can create it

Love can't bring us happiness
But happiness can bring us to love
Power can't bring us happiness
But happiness can show us power

On the line of what is real and
What really isn't
Dream for happiness
Somewhere between heart and mind
The spirit of life can be seen
Happiness comes in a way to dream

Material Junkies

Material junkies hold out hands
Praying hard for a better deal
Card holder smiles and shuffles away
His luck just gets better each day

Somewhere between darkness and light
A shadow where nothing knows right
Some place at the cross and a dream
Someone is dirty the image unclean

In the act of one way or another
Junkie needle ravages the mother
Rationalized minds craving the high
Progressive race is choking the sky

Crooked eyes seeing only crooked fears
Waters song plays to deaf ears
Yesterdays child betrays
Tomorrows child
Chasing a fix that only lasts
For a while

Held breath awaits the next move
Lightning dancer is laying the groove
Cool thunder comes riding the flash
Becoming a storm predator can't pass

Within the grasp of the fiery feather
There is a thread
That pulls it together
In the chasm between motive and intent
There is a thread
That pulls it together

Some People Say

Some people say we are born
Some people say we enter this world
Some people say we die
Some people say we continue on

There are crazed humans out there
They exist mad as in possessed
Something is nothing never enough
They forgot how to be fair

Crazed humans want to own everything
No matter what they have to do
Money and things become their drug
Driven not caring about being
In madness crazed humans
Poisoning the water and the air
Disrespecting the mother

Crazed humans going nowhere
Children of earth be careful
Doing one's best is very good
Mistakes are part of the lesson

We are sunshine and clouds
We are water in rivers flow
Remember the mother
Crazed humans forgot her

Crazed humans speak of me and mine
Disregarding the us we and ours
Propagandizing not to care
Brainwashing not to share

Some people say we enter this world
Some people say we continue on

One Journey

Moths and other sacred wings
Butterflies and bees whisper
In breath of the wind
Blessed way blessing way things

Dreams are the minds streams
Thought pictures of the spirit
There are dreams of the day
There are dreams of the night

Thinking and dreaming are related
Dreams of the day we make our own
Dreams of night part of eternals stone
There are dream takers
Taking from dream worlds
Taking dreams as a way of
Stealing thoughts

Turning minds inside then out
Dream slavers want to change
Our connections to ourselves
Mess with our dreams make us unsure
Unclear about right and wrong
Feed our dreams and instincts
To industrial profit machine

Difference between dream and fantasy
Reality and illusion center and no center
Dreams of the day keep our spirit alive
Our creative mind who we really are

With dreams we can create and heal
Follow our original purpose
Dreams are protection good medicine
Blessed way blessing way things

Sun and moon continue
We are all on one journey

Child of the Dream

Never really told the truth
Never really told a lie
Never really did know why

In the land of diminishing faces
Thought heads into nowhere places
Souls with holes grab for a proper mask
Lives in roles succumb to the task

Some good things don't get done
With everyone delaying everyone
Life lights the fires of every spirit
But some bodies are too torn to hear it

Never really told the truth
Never really told a lie
Never really did know why

Predator infects in a predator way
Diseasing intentions of the DNA
Slaying spirits with obedience rules
Capturing minds with mind control tools

Everywhere the wind sings in a song
Don't let illusion feed you
To the machine
There's time to be clear
Time to be strong
We are the child
The child of the dream

Never really told the truth
Never really told a lie
Never really did know why

Peace with Earth

Longing eyes long for more
More to life more to living
More to love more than this
Daily grinds wear at worn souls
Clocks tell of times running
Free world peoples wearing masks
No one's recognized who's inside
The distance is how everyone feels

New world orders submissive minds
Warmakers new old rules
Authorities are to be obeyed
There is proper behavior's face
Questions are not to be
Different is bad when it's you
Good boys and girls do as they're told
Bad boys and girls go straight to hell
Thoughts wearing a coat of one color
Isolations desperate to be happy

In the wilderness life continues
Water and land sustainers of life
All our relations call to us
Ancestral spirit reaches to longing eyes
But some longing eyes can't see to feel
Suns moons and stars tell of times
Natural world beauty shows itself
Recognition and energies flow in power
In no distance all things are related
Children of earth with earth mother
Circle of life
What goes around comes around

Responsible human beings
Act accordingly
Giving and caring or love and aggression
Within the circle or outside the circle
There is no peace without peace with earth
Peace with our mother peace with ourself
Peace with earth is our power
Peace with earth   peace

Johnny Damas and Me

1994

When I went down these roads
it wasn't for glory or gold
it was just to keep going

Rant 'n' Roll

See the Woman

Raptor

Shadow over Sisterland

Baby Dolls Blues

That Love

Johnny Damas and Me

Across My Heart

Something about You

After All These Years

All There Is to It

Rant 'n' Roll

Welcome to graffiti land
All the rides are in your head
The ticket is what is thought
And what is said
Our attitudes are climbing
We don't have time for more mind-wasting lies
Whatever it is you're doing we're not going to buy it
It's time to say something not a time to be quiet

Rant and roll heartspeak from the spirit
Say it loud so everyone can hear it
Say what you mean   mean what you say
Rant and roll when you feel that way

Religions of men heavy with fear
Industrial war against the land
Every woman knows the fugitive
Rich men keep living off the poor
The soul is what's left after they eat your spirit
When every act is an act of self-defense
We have to do something or perish in the pretense

In this together and on our own
A reality of how we feel
Either we can dance with someone
Or we can dance alone
A plurality of sight and view
We and us are me and you

Predator views are way too tragic
Mother Earth gives us power
Father Sky makes us magic
Life doesn't have to be bitter
Even when its not always sweet
Synchronicity is the rendezvous
When magic and power meet

Rant and roll heartspeak from the spirit
Say it loud so everyone can hear it
Say what you mean   mean what you say
Rant and roll when you feel that way

See the Woman

She has a young face an old face
She carries herself well in all ages
She survives all man has done

In some tribes she is free
In some religions she is under man
In some societies she is worth what she consumes

In some nations she is delicate strength
In some states she is told she is weak
In some classes she is property owned

In all instances she is sister to earth
In all conditions she is life bringer
In all life she is our necessity

See the woman eyes
Flowers swaying on scattered hills
Sun dancing calling in the bees

See the woman heart
Lavender butterflies fronting blue sky
Misty rain falling on soft wild roses

See the woman beauty
Lightning streaking dark summer nights
Forests of pines mating with new winter snow

See the woman spirit
Daily serving courage with laughter
Her breath a dream
And a prayer

Raptor

Raptor I am craving you
A way my mind feels
This feeling of about you
Yearns me
A way my heart thinks
The thought of without you
Burns me

These heavy heat blues
Craving you
Some fires I know
These heavy heat blues

A thousand full moons
Pound in my heart
Craving you wanting to be
Wild with you
Wild with you

Craving you
I'll give you kisses anytime
In the story of the moment
The color of your eyes
Sweet heart dreams

Playing with the night
We are the child of matches
We are the child of matches
Playing with the night

Craving you
Water on fire
Drenching the sun
You make the rain sizzle

Clenching my soul
In a devotion to you
Thrilling my heart
Thrilling my heart

Raptor
Pretty like a smile
Lingering like a while
In the whirl
My mind goes different
Once I was on nobody's side
Now I am wanting
To see with you
What love will do

Craving you
A thousand full moons
Pound in my heart
Wanting to be
Wild with you
Wild with you

Raptor I am craving you

Shadow over Sisterland

There's a shadow over sisterland
With a Smith and Thomas
Pointed at her head
Pointed at her head
Money and authority
Have their own way of talking
Their own way of talking
When it comes to the man
Versus what the woman said
Versus what the woman said
There's a shadow there's a shadow
There's a shadow over sisterland

Somewhere sometimes
A woman lives the memory
Of the little girl's pain
Dragging through the mind
Dragging through the time
Every day a compromise
Just to do the time
Just to do the time
Silence is a mask
Silence is a mask

When nothing can be said
When nothing can be said
There's a shadow there's a shadow
There's a shadow over sisterland

Goddess gave the chalice
Dominator made the blade
God slew the serpent
And the woman's bed was made

Tethers of chains
Tethers of jewels
Economic bondage
Runs by those rules
The laws of justice
Are business decisions
Gender and class
Cut with surgical precision
Religious definition
And the politics of man
Church and state together
Hand in hand
There's a shadow there's a shadow
There's a shadow over sisterland

Mother Earth as goddess
Is woman meets the god of men
Violent prayers rationalizing madness
Partnership comes to an end
Landlords
Landlords
Landlords
Ownership prevails ownership prevails
Ruling class industrial male

Ruling class industrial male
Ruling class industrial male
There's a shadow there's a shadow
There's a shadow over sisterland

Goddess gave the chalice
Dominator made the blade
God slew the serpent
And the woman's bed was made

There's a shadow over sisterland

Baby Dolls Blues

In a cosmos of temptations leanings
All that went down had many meanings
She saw some light hidden behind the dark
In rivers of loneliness anger left its mark
Many of lifes chapters written by wrong doing men
Gambling to win her desperation not to lose again

A woman holds remnants of girl childs goals
Wandering through dimensions of wandering souls
Much more pain than glory as her story unfolds
The reality is the illusion keeps playing roles
Late night sleeping dreams still coming back
A mind with the blues wearing mourning black

Baby dolls blues a girl now all grown up
The golden chalice turns into a Teflon cup
Playhouse dreams devoured by livings scenes
Everything's something with nothing as it seems

Gnawing pain aching from long time hurt
Suppression memory reflections self-worth
There's a noisy closet behind a locked door
Filled with a past that can't take any more
Searching for the key to let her run free
Life beyond the image see another reality

In love with a man so slow to learn
Standing her ground no more cheeks to turn
Cages were built by what's been done
This sister a prisoner living under the gun
Standing accused she cries that's not me
I'm a real person   why why won't you see

Needing the peace she's searching for
Worn down from those days at war
With private truths she wants to tell
But she doesn't want to be put through hell
When she finds a love that can understand
She'll be free   having found a promised land

That Love

Don't want that love
No more to me
Baby it's the fire
That burns my tears

Out living my life
The road of no turning back
Part of the art
Is knowing how not to use
Maybe we didn't play the same
Whatever the same may be
Don't want that love

Ways I've been feeling
Got to talk about pain
You know the kind
Got ways of running
Running through the brain
Don't want that love

It's a noisy world
And I'm part of the noise
When it's a quiet world
I'm part of the quiet
What world am I in

It's not what we did
It's what we didn't do
We didn't fill our expectation
We didn't fit our description
No more to me

Your demons sing like angels
I followed the song
Facing suns from shadows
Heart beats were my speed

I built an unintentional corral
From the center however I move
That fence keeps closing in
Feigning calm wants to break out
Flung into the universe

Don't want that love
No more to me
Baby it's the fire
That burns my tears
The road of no turning back
Don't want that love
No more to me

Johnny Damas and Me

Johhny Damas and me
And the mongrel dog the mongrel dog
We've been laying real low
Laying real low in the shadow of the road
Shadow of the road   the road to success
The road to success we stood face to face
Face to face   we went head to head
Head to head   over the idea of money
The idea of money the idea of money
And that's the way it's done
And that's the way it's done
And that's the way it's done
Speaking in tongues
Speaking in tongues phrases and traces
Traces of words traces of words
Something still doesn't settle
Still doesn't settle   still doesn't settle
Still …

Wild wine on a coyote moon
High on a hill   high on a hill
A reckless wind knocks
A reckless wind knocks
Rattling the night rattling the night

In a home not his own
Over his shoulder over his shoulder
Watching the door watching the door
Ready for flight ready for flight
Needing to run needing to run needing to run

In the Nazi Babylon
In the Nazi Babylon in the Nazi Babylon
Lucifer dances with angels
Dances with angels dances with angels
And the dead and the dead
Carry the living on their backs
On their backs on their backs

In the Nazi Babylon
In the Nazi Babylon in the Nazi Babylon
Ruthless and arrogant
Ride the pale pony ride the pale pony
Using hatred as a shield
Hatred as a shield hatred as a shield
In the world where to give
Also means to take also means to take
Also means to take someones must yield
Someones must yield someones must yield
In the Nazi Babylon in the Nazi Babylon
In the Nazi Babylon

Johnny Damas and me yeah Johnny and me
From the story of love the story of love
And prove that you love me
Prove that you love me prove that you love me
A broken heart
I couldn't recognize couldn't recognize
And the mongrel dog the mongrel dog
The mongrel dog went mad in the arms

Mad in the arms mad in the arms
Of many lovers many lovers many lovers
They wept in the high
Baby don't cry baby don't cry
Baby don't cry love like the wind
Love like the wind fly baby fly
Fly baby fly fly baby fly

And the man who is a ghost
Is a ghost
Is a ghost
Is an ally of mine
An ally of mine
An ally of mine
He saw the whole thing
He saw the whole thing

From where I can see
From where I can see
Too bad for Johnny and them
Yeah poor Johnny and them
From what I can see
From what I can see
This can't happen to me
Can't happen to me
Can't happen to me
I don't carry it well
Don't carry it well
Don't carry it well

And the man who is a ghost
Is a ghost
Is a ghost
Is an ally of mine
Is an ally of mine

Johnny Damas and me
And the mongrel dog
The mongrel dog
We been laying real low

Across My Heart

Your eyes magnet fire
A hideout in the night
There are memories
You are one of the wonders
Finishing touches
Moccasin tracks
Across my heart

Your eyes spirit flame
Some things words
Can't explain
Thinking of you to me
Not to possess but as part of
Like my liberty my heart my soul
Parts of me
Moccasin tracks
Across my heart

There are smiles and whiles
I can't get past
You are my other self
Finishing touches
Moccasin tracks
Across my heart

Sort of like a courting
The color of my heart
Rhinestone Indian
The sparkle is inside of me
Problem with this love
I can't love you long enough
Most distant star is too close
Compared to time I need
Moccasin tracks
Across my heart

Your eyes natural heat
Fire in my dream
In the light I can see
We are the fire
The light is you and me
Moccasin tracks
Across my heart

There are smiles and whiles
I can't get past
You are my other self
Finishing touches
Moccasin tracks
Across my heart

Something about You

There's something about you
Runs fire through my heart
Something about you
A waiting oasis

I saw you again
Seems like it's been too long
I think you noticed
It was good to hear you
Inspirations
You make my heart beat fast
Reminding me of a thought
I want to unfold you
And wear the night

There are days of glory
Smiling light
Sounds of you weave
Into sounds yet to come
Dreamer eyes love stars
Casting soft heat
You looked good
I looked twice

Something about you
Runs fire through my heart
Something about you
A waiting oasis
Fertile soil to be tilled
Reaching for magician's wand
Wanting to be the good seed
I ride a gentle wind

Fire through my heart
Reminding me of a thought
I want to unfold you
And wear the night

Breathtaking excitement
Just knowing you're around
This good feeling firestorm
One with one with the universe
My mind flies very very high
Your beauty has power
That's as good as it gets
I can't ask for more

There's something about you

After All These Years

After all these years
The last time I saw you
Is only a moment away
As always
I reach for your touch
Only to find
I'm teardrops behind

Falling from a rising star
I chase a changing sun
Sunshine seems so far
In this distance I have to run

All these years
Inside my head
I dance the dance
Of sorrows heart
And little memories
Are precious jewels
Reminding me
Of where and when

Laughter wasn't a shadow
And the shadow
Wasn't this cold

Falling from a rising star
I chase a changing sun
Sunshine seems so far
In this distance I have to run

The last time I saw you
I loved the wind
When she was a woman
A woman went away
Every time this time
Comes around
Some ghosts that haunt
Are a plague or a blessing
In this my heart of want

After all these years
And after all these tries
The man I am
Is only the remains
Of reasons and logics
I don't understand
Every time I allow my mind
To think of or dwell on you
I sure miss you
After all these years
Nothing changes that
After all these years
The next time I see you
After all these years

Falling from a rising star
I chase a changing sun
Sunshine seems so far
In this race I have to run

All There Is to It

All there is to it
We can't take we can't pay
We can't say any more

All there is to it
We went to the emperors ball
The emperor sang
A song about sacrifice
A song about sacrifice
Sacrifice who sacrifice what
Sacrifice you sacrifice me
The altar of democracy
The altar of democracy
The altar of democracy
Sacrifice who sacrifice what
Sacrifice you sacrifice me
The altar of democracy
The altar of democracy
The altar of democracy
Sacrifice you sacrifice you
Sacrifice you sacrifice me

Big business decision big business decision
Big business decision maximizing profit
Maximizing profit maximizing profit
Third world labor third world labor
Third world labor it's cheaper that way
It's cheaper that way it's cheaper that way

Big business decision big business decision
Big business decision savings and loan
Savings and loan savings and loan
Trillion dollar debt
Trillion dollar debt trillion dollar debt
And there's taxman at the door
Taxman at the door taxman at the door
Telling me I gotta pay telling me I gotta pay
Telling me I gotta pay

Bankerman
Bankerman bankerman
Has the deed to the land
The deed to the land
The deed to the land
And the thieves got away
And the thieves got away
And the thieves got away

The altar of democracy
The altar of democracy
The altar of democracy
Sacrifice who sacrifice what
Sacrifice you sacrifice me
Sacrifice you sacrifice me

The altar of democracy
There's richman richman
Richman   richman
Behind god and the flag
Behind god and the flag
Behind god and the flag
Richman
Behind god and the flag

Behind god and the flag
Richmans taking more
Richmans taking more
Richmans taking more
And the poor and the poor
And the poor get more poor
More poor more poor

The altar of democracy
The altar of democracy
Sacrifice who sacrifice what
The altar of democracy

All there is to it all there is to it
We don't believe what you say
We don't believe what you say
We don't believe what you say
It doesn't have to happen like this
It doesn't have to happen like this
It doesn't have to happen like this

We don't accept what you say
We don't accept what you say
We don't accept what you say
We won't roll over for you
We won't roll over for you
We won't roll over for you
All there is to it
All there is to it
The altar of democracy
The altar of democracy
Sacrifice who
Sacrifice what

And the thieves got away
And the thieves got away
And the thieves got away

The altar of democracy

Blue Indians

1999

Have you ever done any time
it's not always a pretty thing
what can go on behind
the walls of your mind

Blue Indians
Bad Dog
All Nite Café
Toy
Devil and Me
Johnny and Joe
Angel of Sin
Terminal Neon
Dizzy Duck
Grassfire
The Only One for Me
You Were

Blue Indians

Thoughts of dreams aren't really dreams
Escaping nothing nothing escapes
Myth slayers undermine their own realities
Feeding turbulence to souls distortion streams
Wearing away inside of hearts worn out
Branded in prisons of fantasy and doubt

Blue Indians being pulled into melting pots
Grueling class rules the haves and have-nots
Industrial reservation tyranny stakes its claim
Blue Indians emotional siege in civilized stain

Shadows forsaken truths unrecognized   tears fall
From broken minds of man aggression masquerades
In many rides   winner takes all a lie that lies
Illusion greed with a respected side
Glory and gold lead a desperate chase

Stranded persons search for meaning
Storykeepers run out of bandages
Histories washed in ritual blood
Traditions bleed in high-tech flood
Workers not serfs terminologies change
Progress as evolution terminal strange

Blue Indians being pulled into melting pots
Grueling class rules the haves and have-nots
Industrial reservation tyranny stakes its claim
Blue Indians emotional siege in civilized stain

Tears fall from broken minds of man
Living carelessly a statement of its own
Bitter fruit emerges where bitter seed is sown
Economic chains all dressed out as reward
Gender race age edged in love and rage
Oppressorman builder keeper of the cage

Blue Indians being pulled into melting pots
Grueling class rules the haves and have-nots
Industrial reservation tyranny stakes its claim
Blue Indians emotional siege in civilized stain

Bad Dog

Bad dog
The places you've never been
The reasons you're weeping for
Tomorrows leftover lies
Layering the scars in your eyes

Bad dog
Man keeps playing at being master
There's a way you're expected to obey
Don't bite the hand that feeds you
Don't you know what freedom means

Bad dog can't escape the heat
Disguised as a memory howling the sky
Always chasing almost love that way
Loaded heart and the need to run
Almost always chasing love that way

Bad dog
Dark in the alone prowling the night
Pulled by a scent in the wind
Too hot to handle to cool to love
The moon keeps calling for you
Bad dog   breathless a hearbeat away
Shaking earth and souls that tremble
Stormy times and broken rhymes
Every chance you take
Leaves behind one you didn't

Bad dog
The cage the cage is full of empty lives
Whatever it is you think you're dreaming
Wherever it is you think you are
This isn't the same world
This isn't the same world
Bad dog

Bad dog
Can't escape the heat
Dark in the alone
Breathless a heartbeat away
Man keeps playing at being master
There's a way you're expected to obey
Don't bite the hand that feeds you
Don't you know what freedom means

Bad dog bad dog

All Nite Café

Tasting the promise
In the want to need
A worn path in the dark
Looking for the all nite café

Playing along with flickering fire
Shadow cloud soulmate of the sun
Good and bad can't decide
Chance dances on the great divide
I broke my heart and I lost my mind
Trying not to run out of time
Coherent extremes stand in the challenge
Incoherent extremes pursue their way
And the middle times
Are the neutrality with no meaning

Tasting the promise
In the want to need
A worn path in the dark
Looking for the all nite café

Sometimes me and my mind
Don't get along very well and
Sometimes I need someone to talk to
And someone to cling to
A little bit of forever for a little while
Doing the rest of the life I can't hide
I fell through some of the wounds
And pulled the scars inside
Fragmented memories are incoming rounds
Blowing my mind more into pieces
Any way is no choice but ride this ride

A worn path in the dark
Looking for the all nite café
Tasting the promise
In the want to need
A worn path in the dark
Looking for the all nite café

Toy

There are reasons
Elusive is elusive
Those reasons know
What they're doing

Then she discovered
Pretty doesn't need the truth
She likes to be looked at
But she doesn't like to be seen

Working the pretty
When to be nice
Just how to do it
Turn it on turn it on

Toy what's in the doing
Is in the way it's done
Those scars that can't be seen
These scars can't be outrun
In the hidden some nightmares
Are a racehorse
Behavioring the fires
With their own life force

Working the pretty
The sincerest of smiles
Personal tones
Little intimacies
A taste of the prize

Wanting to be wanted
Close almost like love
Serious toys the games of men
Make believe daddys and
Uncles of pretend
The scent of used lovers
And new made friends
Yearning calls out desire
Desire answers the call

Some ways of getting even
Keep using up self-esteem
She likes to be looked at
But she doesn't like to be seen

Working the pretty
Some things never change
Working the pretty
When to be nice
Just how to do it
Turn it on turn it on

Working the pretty
She likes to be looked at
But she doesn't like to be seen

Working the pretty

Devil and Me

Better leave me be baby
Can't you see baby
The devil and me baby
Been around too long baby
Nothing's all right baby
My light went wrong baby
The dark makes night baby
It's nothing you done baby
It's the way I run baby
It's the way I run baby
It's the way I run baby

Stones through the glass baby
Cracks in the wall baby
Clouds instead of sun baby
Crazy like a man baby
Love sharper than the knife baby
Confusion the trail of my life baby
Regret in the palm of my hand baby
What I don't remember baby
I can't let it go baby
Something to what I did baby
What I don't want to know baby
History of my stories baby
Endings tattered glories baby

Baby look at you baby
Been through a mill of your own baby
You've seen some sad times too baby
Still there's a good life for you baby
No real need to rush baby
Just be careful what you do baby
I can see in your eyes baby
You've been a victim before baby
Of people like the devil and me baby

The devil and me baby
Baby can't you see baby
The devil and me baby
It's nothing you done baby
It's the way I run baby
It's the way I run baby
It's the way I run baby
Run baby run baby
Run baby run

Johnny and Joe

Johnny and Joe out behind the back door
Drinking from a brown paper bag
Smooth stories telling their lives
Talking about times of love and war
Two alley cats passing some time

Where they could've been with the right breaks
Seems life didn't trust them to succeed
Some other guys have all the luck
Two friends partners to the end
Passing brown paper bag around

Along came pretty Lu showing her style
Flashing her eyes flashing some leg
Hard-working girl needs to unwind
One's going to get lucky she needs a man
Likes them both but she's not that kind
Something to give who will she choose

Johhny and Joe out behind the back door
Drinking from a brown paper bag
Smooth stories telling their lives
Talking about times of love and war
Two alley cats passing some time

From sunrise 'til dawn
Evening the score
Sunset doesn't end
When the bottles at war
Feeling good and bad feelings
Dance strange in minds
That are reeling
How quickly time flies
Between the mouth and the glass

Pretty Lu said to Johnny you're so cute
Said to Joe oh you're so strong
Johnny reached for pretty Lu
Joe went for his gun shots to the night
Brown paper bag drops to the ground
Bloody wine in sudden ending
Poor pretty Lu
Never did get to unwind

Angel of Sin

The angel of sin
Kept knocking at my door
So I thought what the hell
Must be time to let this angel in
Let this angel in the angel of sin

A way fast fire runs
Hotter than lust in hell
I knew I was still alive
Or feeling real good dead
The angel of sin the angel of sin

A way she broke it down
She told to me she told to me
I'm the angel you can trust
It's cupid who's armed
She told to me she told to me
The angel of sin

She told to me she told to me
Is it love over like
Is it lust over love
I really didn't know   but
Was willing for all three
Something for this angel and me
This angel and me
The angel of sin

She told to me she told to me
If you want to see
It's best you learn
The truth of the lie
What you weave
Is what you wear
And the story on hate
Hate needs love
And love needs
To be understood

She told to me she told to me
The temptation rules
If you're going to play
It's best you live every day
To understand what you're living
It's best you know how you're giving
She told to me she told to me

The angel of sin
Kept knocking at my door
So I thought what the hell
Must be time
To let this angel in

Let this angel in
The angel of sin

Terminal Neon

Feeling a little imposed upon
And a whole lot unneeded
In walked Lucifer himself
Wearing mismatched faded black
Reflecting some hard times of his own

Terminal neon
Unsurrealistically real
As they keep slipping
Back into the familiar
Broken dreams the falling tears
Everybody feels but nobody hears
In the democratization of the sheep
The white sheep don't trust the black sheep
And it's all the shepherds idea

Terminal neon
The third world war
The third world is poor
The third world war
Against the poor
All over the world
The ruling class rich
The third world war
Against the poor

Terminal neon
Human weakness turned
Addictions and other needing crimes
Battlegrounds littered with self-respect
Rage and frustration the real desperation
Serial killers become the high priest
In the culture of death without ritual

Terminal neon
The angel of mercy
Hasn't been showing much mercy these days
The have-nots want it need it pray for it
What the little things mean
Everything all adds up
Human beings voided humanoids
Terminal neon it's all very strange

Feeling a little imposed upon
And a whole lot unneeded
In walked Lucifer himself
Wearing mismatched faded black
Reflecting some hard times of his own

Dizzy Duck

Dizzy duck blood brother
To like-minded Sam
Every day a little small duck
Walked by the big and tall shop
For big and tall men
How he wanted but he just
Couldn't go in

So depressing for poor Dizzy
He had to impress himself
He went to another store to
Buy himself a gun
The gun store man said let's
See some ID
Says Dizzy I don't need any
I'm a duck
Oh yeah says the gun store man
So Dizzy bought himself his gun
Nothing like a gun
To make a duck feel like a man
His very own gun
How he loved his very own gun
Dizzy liked life with his very own gun
Pretty soon his gun was his very best friend
He loved his gun so much   he got another
One
He didn't want his gun to get lonely
When he had to leave it all alone
Like when he went to the airport
Or when he went ducknizing

One day after every day of
Walking
By the store for big and tall men
Dizzy couldn't take it anymore
He went home and got his very own gun
And his other one
Dizzy and his guns on the street
In front of the store for big and tall men

Dizzy and his other gun opened fire
Shooting down people right and left
No remorse what's a people to a duck
But when his other gun was empty
Dizzy knew what was coming
If he stuck around

Right there on the street
In the blood and screams
Dizzy ate his very own gun
Like a lollipop he put it to his lips
In a strange nipple ritual
Dizzy sucked his life away
Blowing the chip off his shoulder
Because some ducks just can't handle it

Anyway this is just a warning
Beware of a duck
Named like-minded Sam

Grassfire

In between the blues
There are good days and bad days
With everything and nothing to lose
While the setting sun never sits
And the night has no limits

The void between freedom and free
Dealing with the unnatural reality
A need to see a need to be
Grassfire my DNA needs THC

In the unnatural society
Been trying to maintain
While the sane appear
To be clearly insane
With no way to explain

Outlasting the great lie
A sparking spark does my mind
Grassfire pulling the sky
Breathing in Sativas design

The void between freedom and free
Dealing with the unnatural reality
A need to see a need to be
Grassfire my DNA needs THC

Dreaming of long times past
All that those times brought
Looking to the heart of tomorrow
Grassfire in a world that yearns
That's the way this fire burns

The Only One for Me

It was that second look   circling fire
That second look   throwing flame
Now I'm the burning tree
You're the only one for me

Without a second thought this way of feeling
A second thought the truth of hearts
Can this be love the question can't be answered
The answer just is you're the only one for me

I've had my struggles with self and worth
There are ways I used to hurt
Now I'll throw that hurt away
Count this blessing a feather from the wind
Moonbeams kissing smile the truth of hearts
You're the only one for me

If you're drawn to me in ways I'm drawn to you
Together we can dream and live that dream
We know what forever is there's no worry there
It's this time we have respecting love
The truth of hearts you're the only one for me

With this second chance the bringing sun
This second chance I'll always love the rain
Those wet nights in the forest fire me down calm me up
You are in my mind think I'll listen
The truth of hearts you're the only one for me

It was that second look   circling fire
That second look   throwing flame
Now I'm the burning tree
You're the only one for me

You Were

You were my prayer my good book
You were my heroin my cocaine
You were my wealth my glory
You were my mystery my answers
You were my today my tomorrow
You were here but not long enough

Pretty woman in my mind
That laughter in my soul
Those memories in my heart
Pretty lonely here left behind

You were my material my desire
You were my reasons my best look
You were my medicine my healing
You were my want my need
You were here but not long enough

You were my teacher my lesson
You were my sanctuary my truth
You were my woman my warmth
You were my ally my love
You were my dream my reality

You were here but not long enough
Pretty woman in my mind
That laughter in my soul
Those memories in my heart
Pretty lonely here left behind

Bone Days

2001

I keep telling myself
the dark
is part of the light

> Crazy Horse
> Other Close Times
> Undercurrent
> Carry the Stone
> Ever Get the Blues
> Lucky Motel
> Bone Days
> Takes My Breath
> Spectator
> Sorry Love
> Nothing in Her Eyes
> Doesn't Hurt Anymore
> Hanging from the Cross

Crazy Horse

Crazy Horse
We hear what you say
One Earth one Mother
One does not sell the Earth
The people walk upon
We are the land
How do we sell our Mother
How do we sell the stars
How do we sell the air

Crazy Horse
We hear what you say
Too many people standing their ground
Standing the wrong ground
Predators face he possessed a race
Possession a war that doesn't end
Children of god feed on children of earth
Days people don't care for people
These days are the hardest
Material fields material harvest
Decoration on chain that binds
Mirrors gold the people lose their minds

Crazy Horse
We hear what you say
One Earth one Mother
One does not sell the Earth
The people walk upon
We are the land

Today is now and then
Dream smokes touch the clouds
On a day when death didn't die
Real world time tricks shadows lie
Red white perception deception
Predator tries civilizing us
But the tribes will not go without return
Genetic light from the other side
A song from the heart our hearts to give
The wild days the glory days live

Crazy Horse
We hear what you say
One Earth one Mother
One does not sell the Earth
The people walk upon
We are the land
How do we sell our Mother
How do we sell the stars
How do we sell the air

Crazy Horse
We hear what you say
Crazy Horse
We hear what you say
We are the seventh generation
We are the seventh generation

Other Close Times

It's easy to be well behaved
When you have no one to play with
It's easy to be well depraved
When you have no one to stay with

It's a triangular world
The dinner bell is ringing
There's no cure for hunger or
Whatever passion is bringing

We can run like the wild
Evading capture and taming
Curious is curiosity's child
Before love is for claiming

Blown up into something at stake
The golden fleece cries
At what the mistakes take
From the light in our eyes

The call of the day
Is the call of the night
Sun and moon light the way
Whatever can happen just might

Craving smiles and laughter
And other close times
More than love we're after
It's all between the lines

It's a triangular world
The dinner bell is ringing
There's no cure for hunger or
Whatever passion is bringing

Undercurrent

Undercurrent
A way heat breathes
Dancing sweet
Our introduction
Was our seduction

When touch touches
Magic from beyond
That electric feeling
The messenger

Smolder and smoke
Glistening into fire
Flame jumping
Igniting the exciting
Dripping from the sun
Torrential recognizing
Memory runs deep wants
Deserts needing hot rain

And the rivers ran
Through crazy into wild
Blooming our eyes
Spirit shining
Desire is paled by this roaring
Fast moving swept into a rush

A reappearing familiar
Weaving heartbeat into light
Overflowing feeling
Happy in the heart

Smolder and smoke
Glistening into fire
And the rivers ran
Through crazy into wild
And the rivers ran
Undercurrent
A way heat breathes

Carry the Stone

Hidden in the beauties of Babylon
A civilized behavorial notoriety
The more evil the empire
The more paranoid the society

Building to the new world order
We're expected to carry the stone
Emperors and the feeding class
Human being, being used up fast

The miners keep on mining
Intelligence is the mother lode
Imagination as an energy source
In this predators way of dining

Defining how and what we think
As we're led to the way to believe
Conditioned reaction we call thought
Our reality rides in how we perceive

In the ways of being lost and alone
Who runs from their doubt and fear
In the mask of everything's normal
Who's not feeling or seeing too clear

Could be we're being programmed
In a way our spirit bleeds
All over our lives, our lives
Become fuel for predator needs

Building to the new world order
We're expected to carry the stone
Emperors and the feeding class
Human being, being used up fast

Hidden in the beauties of Babylon
A civilized behavorial notoriety
The more evil the empire
The more paranoid the society

Ever Get the Blues

Did you ever get the blues
Where dreams and reality collided
And you fell through the hole
In your soul finding yourself
Looking for something you lost
And you don't know what it is

Days and nights are months and years
With those can't lose the blues, blues
Dragging you in and out
Of the looking glass
The land of desperate hearts
And wandering souls
Tearing at your mind
Did you ever get the blues
Did they ever get you

Where the sky fell
Pulling all the stars down on you
Leaving only vast darkness
A world where you no longer understood
Searching the eyes of people around you
Seeing that they didn't see it
So where does that leave you
With those can't lose the blues, blues

Breaking the looking glass
Forgetting which world you're in
Surrounded in the density of slowing light
Isolation kindling separated from the spark
Watching flame turn into embers
Knowing that's the promise of your life

Did you ever get the blues
Did you ever say it and
No one could hear you
Did you ever get the blues
Those can't lose the blues, blues
Did they ever get you

Lucky Motel

During times of shadow
In the background of burst
The sun waits for the moon
To torch the night   torch the night

In the broken neon and faded light
The lucky motel at the corner of
Nowhere and the past where memories go
To forget   to forget

Laughing to erase   her name is Lacy
She makes his crazy kinda crazy
His name is Want she can hear it
She wants want but doesn't want to
Sparks of the stars burnings
Strong heat he is like flame
As her fire waits she is a pulse   a pulse
In the charging light as a passion of storm
Fiery rain lightning carries thunder

She's a good girl
Coming to understand
That sometimes this is
What good girls do
What good girls do
In the breath of sighs
In the magic of moan
They held them together
So as not to feel so alone

During times of shadow
In the background of burst
The sun waits for the moon
To torch the night
Torch the night
In the breath of sighs
In the magic of moan
They held them together
So as not to feel so alone

Bone Days

Bone days
The great search for truth
Every meaning has a meaning
Dark and light have their reasons
Live and learn are the seasons

Bone days
With all that's left
Motions of everydayness
And thoughts that won't leave
Leaving behind another sameness
Bone days
When all that's gone
Brings life to your knees
You don't know what to pray
So you keep making pleas

Bone days
What love has to do
Could be no more than
Karma paybacks or karma rewards
Hearts   of wants hearts   of swords
Bone days
In the great need
There is no more enough
Everywhere chasing the chase
Holding and taking play rough

Bone days
The promise is the lie
Someones want to hear
What if the truth is seen
And nobody's living here
Bone days
Covering the night
In the tears of the stars
And the way memories run
Every ending has just begun

Takes My Breath

Takes my breath
Brought me her pretty
And a heart full of yes
The substance of beauty
Gladdening my heart in a
Balance that breathes

Takes my breath
Through spirit and flesh
She comes from the place
Babies go when babies dream
Like a gift of many kisses
A baby dream of my own

Appreciation plus
Temptations wild longing
In expressions of the heart
She's the words
I've been searching for

The scent of lightning
The sweet and the hot
In full woman bloom
She loves me the way
A woman loves
When a woman loves

Some kind of enchanting
I can't get enough
Of getting enough
Destiny is the reality closest
To this feeling she puts on me

Beyond forever a spell is cast
Part her part me   mixed in next
To what forever brings
Takes my breath
Brought me her pretty
And a heart full of yes

Spectator

I'm just a spectator here
Times of transcending time
I should've done what I could
But went and did what I would

In the way angels kiss
We have this time around
Comes back to this, where
We're going is how we're bound

Don't be playing games
That'll start me playing too
The way shadows cross the line
I may have played more games than you

The dormant violence
Of the subtle mind
Makes the cleanest cut
The hardest cut to find

That part where anger alone
Can't keep its promises of revenge
It takes the dance with rage
To put fire to that page

When the laughing and the living
Play it down   it plays out
To the dying and the crying
And whatever is left out

I'm just a spectator here
Times of transcending time
I should've done what I could
But went and did what I would

Sorry Love

After anywhere we've ever been
Left with nothing left to play
Saying we'll never do that again
Another thing we have to say

From our bouquet of hearts
Into dead and dying flowers
Love and sorry are words we use
In this sorry love of ours

In the chaos of our emotions
We've done all we can do
This way we keep dealing
How we feel what we're feeling
You keep saying I'm sorry
And I keep saying it too
Well if this is love then
Maybe it's love that's through

The sound of fear and blame
Crying out a calling name
While this anger keeps giving birth
All those sorrys lose their worth
The storm in our calm
In a planting of seeds
The quantity of our wants
Affects the quality of our needs
Love clashing over love
Playing strength as weakness
Turning pleasuring into pain
In a circling incompleteness

From our bouquet of hearts
Into dead and dying flowers
Love and sorry are words we use
In this sorry love of ours
We've already gone
Everywhere we can go   all we
Need now some nice days in a row

Nothing in Her Eyes

Spoken anger silent hurt
Some kind of wheel
Inside her head going around
And around inside her heart

Heated passions
Chilling effects
When they first met
She couldn't forget
Time's only purpose
Was for them together
They talked together
And were gentle
They laid together
And were flame
She told him her dreams
Trusting him with her prayers
She needed a friend she needed a man

Inside her head going around
And around and around and around

As newness stretches thin
Turns out he didn't understand
Part of the man let her down
Part of the man couldn't give
Part of the man he never was
Part of the man part of her life
Been all through this before

Inside her heart going around
And around and around and around

Heated passions chilling effects
Now here she is
Acting tough again
Turning herself off fast
Curtains dropping in place
Giving away nothing in her eyes

Spoken anger silent hurt
Some kind of wheel
Inside her head going around
And around and around and
Around and around and around
And around and around and around
Inside her heart

Heated passions chilling effects
Now here she is
Acting tough again
Turning herself off fast
Curtains dropping in place
Giving away nothing in her eyes

Doesn't Hurt Anymore

I think about how I'm doing
But I don't know what I'm thinking
Shattering into shadowlight
Reflecting thoughts I can't relieve

My heart doesn't hurt anymore
But my soul does   maybe
That's what souls are for   to
Take the hurt the heart can't take

Distance playing tag playing tricks
With whatever it is I can't find
My weaknesses are my Band-Aids
Covering for how I don't bleed

In all the stones I threw
Some were for flinging
Some were for bringing
And some I never knew

My heart doesn't hurt anymore
But my soul does   maybe
That's what souls are for   to
Take the hurt the heart can't take

Living painted into a picture
Dripping off all these paintings
The colors of emotion
Seeking any kind of devotion

Some things are private
Between me and the dead
And some of the rest
Is better off left unsaid

My heart doesn't hurt anymore
But my soul does   maybe
That's what souls are for   to
Take the hurt the heart can't take

Hanging from the Cross

We weren't lost and
We didn't need any book
Then the great spirit
Met the great lie

Indians are Jesus
Hanging from the cross
Hanging from the cross
In the name of their savior
Forcing on us
The trinity of the chain
Guilt sin and blame
The trinity of the chain
Guilt sin and blame
Hanging from the cross
Hanging from the cross
In a delusional grandeur
They lie to us then
Lie to themselves
About lying to us
Hanging from the cross

Hanging from the cross
In the name of the mother
The child and the human spirit
Indians are Jesus
Hanging from the cross
Hanging from the cross

Hanging from the cross
Hanging from the cross
Damnation or salvation
Among the
Terrorisms of freedom

A civilizing process
Where the rule of law
Is the law of rule
The law is a lie the law is a lie

Hanging from the cross
Hanging from the cross
Their ego empire
The ethnic rich
Their cruelty of class
Imitation opulence
Crumbs that look
Like cake to the masses
Cake to the masses

Hanging from the cross
Hanging from the cross
We don't care
Who they think they are
They look like
Treaty makers to us
Making one more promise
So they'll have
Another promise to break
Another promise to break
Hanging from the cross
Hanging from the cross
They keep asking us
What's wrong with us
We keep saying back
What's wrong with you
Is what's wrong with us

Hanging from the cross
Hanging from the cross
Indians are Jesus
Hanging from the cross
Hanging from the cross
In the name of the mother
The child and the human spirit
Indians are Jesus
Hanging from the cross
Hanging from the cross
We weren't lost
And didn't need any book

Madness and

2007

Whatever it is
you might be needing
it doesn't involve me
I'm too occasional for that

Madness and
Like Temptation
Broke the Light
How Does Tomorrow Dream
Looking for an Angel
Happy Fell Down
Teddy Bear Tears
Waiting for Yesterday
Sweeting the Light
Famine in the Plenty
Asking the Wind
Material Junkies
A Face on God
God Help and Breed You All

Madness and

Madness and chasing the mundane
Between the scarring of dreams
Racing against daytimes nightmares
Trying to put that bad road behind

Here it is already tomorrow afternoon
While the clock claims it's still yesterday
Too many games played in too many heads
So many questions but nothing gets said

Fear teaches denial how not to think
Distorting feelings as a way not to feel
The need to believe shoots up its fix
Scoring with promises when the lie doesn't work

With more tears in our eyes than stars
Civilized cruelty's disguise of rationalization
Elitist class, racist, sexist rage
Chains of freedom and a crack in the liberty bell

Wounds without scars, scars without wounds
Darkening the heart in an isolation of time
In the shadows alone is the hunter
Love without love looks for love to survive

Madness and the sane part of insane
Could it be that just to survive or exist
When viewed through the prism of light
Can be considered a lower form of life

Like Temptation

You look like temptation
I feel like sin
Whatever this is
I'm ready to begin

In a dream urge
Luscious cool delicious heat
Inside this soaring
Let me come to you
If you hear it too

Smoldering
Liquid kisses
Glorifying desire
Bringing many smiles
Warmth to fire

Holding the hot
In the sweet
Rhyming the moment
Poetry and the poem
Two hearts one beat

In a burning
Craving craves need
And need just needs
What we want most
Pulling in all the close

This shelter of longing
A little bit healing
Erasing the numb
Flame consuming pain
Passioning feeling

Broke the Light

Time has ways of running long
But time is only a dimension
Then someone broke the light
Between what's right and wrong

Don't it make you want to cry
Don't it make you want to scream
We've had all we're ever going to have
And lost those dreams we were going to dream

Then someone broke the light
Shaking the sky shaking our soul
Don't it make you want to cry
Make you want to cry

There was pain bleeding from our eyes
But we do what we have to do
We can't promise we had no idea
What we did led to what we're going through

The passion of want, the passion of need
The passion to love, the passion to hate
The passion of passion, the passion to live
The passion of destiny, the passion of fate

We believe we love we love we believe
Then come those cracks in our world
Shaking the sky, shaking our soul
New wounds on scars that are old

If we could take it back what would we take
And what about that part that says to forgive
When the mirror looks at us who do we see
And how did we get ourselves into this reality

Then someone broke the light
Shaking the sky shaking our soul
Don't it make you want to cry
Make you want to cry

How Does Tomorrow Dream
(cowritten with Ricky Eckstein)

In humanities name
At the alters of life
In the temples of greed
The manufacturers of war
God wars to believe in
In a blending of they into we
Using religion to justify killing
Hiding behind god
Implying its god
Who's on a killing spree

Don't wanna get on no airplane
And run it into the ground
Don't wanna start no fires
And burn this world down
Don't understand what we're doing here
It doesn't make much sense
For love of god and oil

They're killing the children in Afghanistan, in
    Ethiopia
They're killing the children in Israel, in Haiti
They're killing the children in Palestine, in the Congo
They're killing all our children

Don't care much for no religion
That tells you who gets to live and die
They fight over their holy lands
Shed blood in the name of their gods
Terrorizing the innocent
The peaceful and the meek
What do they think they are doing here
What do they think

We're killing the children in Iran and Iraq, in Sudan
We're killing the children in north Africa, in Beslan
We're killing the children in America, in Chechnya
We're killing all our children

We teach them how to hate
We teach them our lies
They learn how to be hungry
They learn how to die

Don't want no part of that
Turning light to gray to dark
Abraham never said
Jesus never said
Mohammed never said
Anything about doing any of this
In the name of god
The ideas of men
The price the heart pays
How does tomorrow dream
How does tomorrow dream

We're killing the children in North Ireland, in Rwanda
We're killing the children in El Salvador, in Cambodia
We're killing the children in South Africa, in Sierra Leone
We're killing the children in Columbia
We're killing the children in Pine Ridge
We're killing the children of the world

Looking for an Angel

Dancing at the edge of neon
Wandering into that dark
Needing a middle between right and wrong
It's all I can do to hold back the light

Starving the night of its beauty
Nightmares can't and don't care
Where reality is a game we play
Nothing is forever nothing gets to stay

Looking for an angel
Searching for what I lost
Amongst the things I miss
An angel's heart an angel's kiss

What used to be and what's meant to be
Memories keep questioning the answers
When fate turns love into a ghost
It's the living who haunt destiny

In the wounding of souls
The rage of scars a bleeding of fears
Knowing nothing is going to get better
And now here I am all out of tears

While yesterday weeps into the past
Tomorrow empties into today
Thoughts pouring shadows on dreams
Pain is the price someones must pay

Don't want justice don't want that lie
When it comes to want what I want
I want revenge but what I need is
Is I need to make the devil cry

Happy Fell Down

Then happy fell down
Broken into pieces of light
Fragments of shattering love
Glimpses of what once was
Overwhelmed by what is and
What if and what could've been

At first it didn't seem like much
But then each stone thrown
Had a cumulative effect
Whether they hit or missed
Each thrown stone became
Part of the wall they built

Turning quarrel into ritual
Losing balance turns habitual
Someones truths
Are someone elses lies
During those wars of scars
Old wounds keeping time
Waging battle in the mind

There is when love is blind
When it opens its eyes
It can disappear
The reality
Of what is happening
Is not diminished   by their
Unwillingness to comprehend
It is them who diminish

Teddy Bear Tears

He was a teddy bear
Doing teddy bear time
In a teddy bear prison
For a teddy bear crime

Never meant to go wrong
But the urge was strong
He offed Barbie dolls
'Cause one strung him along
He loved her madly
But she ran around with Ken
He didn't like to lose
His compulsion was to win
It all got out of control
Way rage usually does
He had his pride
She made a fool of who he was

Teddy bear tears
This bear didn't mean to turn bad
Living in a room
With a little girl who had bad dreams
Learning about life and love

Came from the TV screens
Between scenes losing track
Of when madness went mad
Let me be your teddy bear
A memory from his head
Guess it doesn't matter
Because the king is dead

He got carried away
Much more than he meant
He saw her face every place he went
Too many Barbies
Once he started no way to stop
A way of triangles
When you fall from the top

It was all too easy
He kept getting away clean
He ran up a score
To three or four dozen or more
An unexplainable rush
Like a powerful dream
He felt like a bear again
Waging an avengers war

Carelessness tripped him up
In pursuit of the high
Jack in the box surprised his act
No way he could lie
One of the parents busted him
With Barbie hair in his fur
A major mess up was in hanging out
Where the Barbies were
No trial no judge no jury
For his capital offense

No one to hear his side
No way to present a defense
A one-way trip to the garbage can
When justice reacted
The executioner's song
In the morning he'll be compacted

Teddy bear tears
This bear didn't mean to turn bad
Living in a room
With a little girl who had bad dreams
Learning about life and love
Came from the TV screens
Between scenes losing track
Of when madness went mad
Let me be your teddy bear
A memory from his head
Guess it doesn't matter
Because the king is dead

Waiting for Yesterday

Racing against time
When time is to ride
Already ahead of the past
Always behind the future
In the going where we're going
Wishing things were different
Is kind of like sitting around
Waiting for yesterday

Waiting for yesterday
With who we could've been
And what we should've done
Dancing the what if, if only dance

Dazed flutters from anyones eyes
When a lie is the truth, truth is a lie
Illusion creates a need to believe
In want, leading to more want

Distraction is a mark of the wound
Desperation is how this wound bleeds
Thoughts feeling isolated and alone
Reaching inward to darken the soul

What already happened is or isn't
Balanced with what happens next
With every thing that is lost
There's something that might be found
While reality takes it all in
The sun shines, the clouds cloud
The stars star, the moon reflects
The ebb and flow of light

Waiting for yesterday
With who we could've been
And what we should've done
Dancing the what if, if only dance

Sweeting the Light

In the rhyme of match
These embers of torch
Sweeting the light
What you do to me

This temptation of heat
Craving your liquid
That deep fire, then
Sweet rushing flame

An embracing of stirring
Your name is the spark
Fire starting this roar
Blazing through my heart

Much is said about love
But love seems too tame
With no way to explain
Our wilding of gentle

The reality of dream
The closeness of close
Melting destiny and fate
What is meant to be

An unraveling of need
This drenching of desire
And it all started
With your smile

Famine in the Plenty

Famine in the plenty
Patience burns quick
Waiting for the rich
But the rich won't hurry
The rich eat us so
The rich don't worry

In the sun's shadow
Water melts into cold
Running rivers of want
Want needs justice
But justice is just ice
In these rivers of want

The stars in the night
Have seen it all
What isn't remembered
Takes time to weep
The soul isn't empty
Yet it feels that way

All those stolen moments
Still searching to belong
The scent of heaven pulls
The prayers of the prey
Feeling something missing
A constant of every day

Confusion in the happy place
The great lie is one
With all the little lies
Edges of breaking dreams
Cutting into other dreams

Asking the Wind

Lapses of remembering
What else can I think
About what can't be undone
About the closet of regrets

While my mind keeps going
Weeping isn't enough and
Crying really is a crying shame
That doesn't have much meaning
In these eruptions of the scars

My heart is looking for a place
These scenes even the hurt hurts
Knowing there is no way out
Time is a bandage that leaks
Glimpses of memories and touch

Then my soul starts falling
Sometimes I sit in the sun
And pray and reach to the stars
Like a drink without a drunk
Or a future without a dream

Today gets farther and farther away
And those things I need to tell you
Have got me talking to the wind
Maybe I'm asking the wind to hold me
Pretending it's you and time doesn't exist

Lapses of remembering
What else can I think
About what can't be undone
About the closet of regrets

Material Junkies

Material junkies hold out hands
Praying hard for a better deal
Card holder smiles and shuffles away
His luck just gets better each day

Somewhere between darkness and light
A shadow where nothing knows right
Some place at the cross and a dream
Someone is dirty the image unclean

In the act of one way or another
Junkie needle ravages the mother
Rationalized minds craving the high
Progressive race is choking the sky

Crooked eyes seeing only crooked fears
Waters song plays to deaf ears
Yesterdays child betrays
Tomorrows child
Chasing a fix that only lasts
For a while

Held breath awaits the next move
Lightning dancer is laying the groove
Cool thunder comes riding the flash
Becoming a storm predator can't pass

Within the grasp of the fiery feather
There is a thread that pulls it together
In the chasm between motive and intent
There is a thread that pulls it together

Somewhere between darkness and light
A shadow where nothing knows right
Some place at the cross and a dream
Someone is dirty the image unclean

Material junkies hold out hands
Praying hard for a better deal
Card holder smiles and shuffles away
His luck just gets better each day

A Face on God

Putting a face on god
Divine madness
These wars between evil
Even good has to hide
The wrath of the righteous
Awakening a dormant mean
Dirty calling itself clean

When an extreme is right
An extreme is left
All that hate is going around
Rage has no time to rest
More than in the thousands dies
When pain comes from the skies

Debris of Palestine and Wall Street
We are all the innocent
Some more than others but
We are all the innocent
While to the lords of war
We're all a way of keeping score

With gods on everybodys side
Spirit knows hard time is coming
Earth dreads the waiting blood
While death makes a list
Who would've ever thought
Virtual reality would come to this

Saying we're only human is incorrect
In reality we're human and being
What's it going to take to see
Maybe the way we acted today
Maybe the way we lived yesterday
Isn't the way creator created us to be

Creator gives us intelligence
It's our protection, medicine, healing
It's the reality we create every day
Our self-worth, our part in humanity
Answers to questions that haven't been ask
Wait for us in clarity and coherency

God Help and Breed You All

No I didn't read in his own write
But I read about the Hardy Boys
Looking for the treasure
Spin and Marty didn't find
Turns out it was Annette

Even Indiana Jones didn't figure it out
In the temple of dooms gloom
Rats eyes casting yellow light
On Star Wars in Linda Lovelace's throat
Even Beethoven rolled over for
Johnny be good
While Chuck sat in a prison cell
Listening to Elvis die in the army
Before Sgt. Pepper went into
A strawberry field
And turned into the walrus
Climbing into a bed for peace
In love with a Japanese woman
Hated by an international YMCA
Ex-Jesus freak
Who blew him off the mountain
Martin dreamed about

While the CIA didn't say anything
Hoping no one would imagine
Psychiatric head doctor connections
Or Manchurian candidates
Warmakers   behavior modification
Master plan   killing men of peace
While the queen of diamonds
Reshuffled the deck
Turning up the Ronalds
Reagan and McDonald

In 1985 the wasps were still
Trying to swarm
In radioactive mushroom clouds
Taking space rides with
Charlie's Angels
Into the black hole that was left
After the Hardy Boys found the treasure
And didn't know what to do
So they sold her
For drugs
Bad acid
Bringing to this reality a clarity
Hard to believe
From sea to shining sea

Profits pissing lives into the
Wall Street urinal
Which I don't want to read
But someday I'm going to read
In his own write

God help and breed you all

The Moremes

2007

In the way these streets
are made for dogging
and chasing the cat
I never did use anyone
    that didn't at least half agree

> The Moremes
> Francis Brown
> Bringing Much
> Tikaan
> Reason to This
> Took a Little Walk
> The Beast
> My Fire
> Cry Your Tears
> With Yesses
> Iktomi
> Make a Chant
> Baby Boom Che

The Moremes

There's me, there's the other me
There's another me, and then
There are the moremes
We've all got a domino to play so
We've been trying to work it out

We don't know how your life turned
Or what all that means
But me and the mes
We're not going back
We've already seen
What we couldn't do

Any skeletons in our closets
Are our own private stash of bones
That scream with no choice, there's
No scream like the next scream
Reducing the present into nothing
While eternity is now not then
Who's divided into what
And how many does that make
There's love that loves, love that fears
Love that possesses, love that needs proof
Where's the love that accepts
Love that likes love that cares

There's no forgetting some realities
Destiny threw at us
And fate wasn't much help
With its way of loading the load
When we didn't have any say
And it was up to us to carry it

In the land where the lie is king
Using fear like glue, pretending
Pretending isn't pretending
At least one of the mes have seen it all
Each and every one of us want the glory
But not a one of us likes the way we fall

Straying is a way of walking
When staying isn't an option
Because we've been accused
Of some things we did and
Somethings we didn't do and
We heard I forgive yous that lied

Me and the mes are looking
For a me that will answer to me
So far there's no one who will

Francis Brown

In the piecing together
Tracing the past
I ran into a shadow
Francis Brown   someone
From a long time back
He doesn't get out much
But when he does
All that he sees is
All that he thinks
And all that he thinks
He thinks to me

He thinks to me
I sat in too many rooms
With the walls staring at me
Looking through everything
All those things I started
And now I can't find

Waiting for the wanting
After the needing
All that enough means
Is no more and sometimes
Some respected the man
Who'd been through everything
But didn't respect
The man going through it

Broken hearts bleeding
All over time and beyond
Love without respect
Love without caring
Love without love
The intensity is the intimacy
Everything else is just confused
Trying to give a better name
To whatever it is we crave

And all that he thinks
He thinks to me

In my addictions
Am I depleting or energizing
I'm crazy, I had to be
Maybe crazy is needed
To protect the coherency
They never knew who I was
They thought I was someone else

I used to think it was about
Knowing what I'm doing
Now sometimes just because
I know, doesn't mean I understand
And sometimes parts of my life
Slipped away in the difference

And all that he thinks
He thinks to me

Different light
In the unloading every halo
I ever touched, I tarnished
The imbalances I made, belong
To me even when I don't get it
And whatever peace I made, counts

When things start falling apart
All I can do is let it fall
When I put it back together
The lesson could be
I can't have it that way so
When I pick up the pieces
Pick up only the pieces I need

Bringing Much

Baby you are my fire
Taking me on a heart run
Warmth heat and flame
Burning holes in the sun

I've been through winter
Chasing way to many storms
And baby I've been part of
That frozen in my heart

Behind a shadow moon
Tears falling to the sky
I heard a sad sad song
That made madness cry

Then I felt your smile
Rushing to my head
I've known you always
In this our little while

Now the stars are shooting
Through my mind into time
The moment of this needing
The chance of this meeting

Dreams of bringing much
I can recognize memories
Forever longing and lingering
Savoring remembering touch

Baby you are my fire
Taking me on a heart run
Warmth heat and flame
Burning holes in the sun

Tikaan

The licorice wolf with neon eyes
And the wolf in wolf's clothing
Appeared in the night of the blue moon

Traveling from the other side of time
They took him beyond self-reflection
Into realities of light as it really is

Dreaming wolf welcomed him
A place of no separation by perception
Into the land where all are people

We are the wolf, you are the wolf
We are the tree, you are the tree
We are the living, you are the living

Mother Earth calls to her children
You are all related is the ingredient
Without it you won't know who you are

Hunted wolf took him by the hand
A little kindness never hurt anyone
A lot of kindness does so much more

Vanishing wolf sang in the sun
There's more to what's going on
Than what's going on

Ghost wolf laughed in ghost wolf way
Your craving shadows are your demise
Listen to the sound of crying when crying cries

Look into our eyes
We are the past
Visiting the future
Look into your mind
What kind of meaning
Do you find

The licorice wolf with neon eyes
And the wolf in wolfs clothing
Appeared in the night of the blue moon

Speaking wolf spoke in words
Distortion plagues from minds of man
You call us predator then make us the prey

Spirit wolf knows lessons of beauty
Beauty's in eyes of the beholder
Reality is in reach of those beholding eyes

Reason to This

Last night in a dream
I interrogated god
Why is it the good die young
What's the reason to this?
We talked we argued, we cried
I never did get any answers
But god knows I tried

The answers already know
A question for the question
Who is it, took the creation story
Claimed it, then took it apart
Glorifying obedience and fear
A rampaging through the mind
Stamping uncertainty into the heart

Then there's that original sin
And something about the devil to pay
And that golden rule do unto others
Obviously isn't really a rule
The lord giveth, the lord taketh away
The violence gets violenter, while
God just sits there with nothing to say

I've read it's said
In the beginning was the word
And the word was god
I've never read it's said
In the beginning was thought
And the thought was think
What that has to do with anything

Took a Little Walk

Me and chaos took a little walk
Down to the abyss had a little talk
Somewhere behind the hurt
Is a demon to deal with

When did the great shock start
In the transparent reality
Waves of walls of fear
Rolling through the psyche

What we can't live with
Lives with us anyway
Soulmelting into confusion
What does this fusion mean

Then look what we did
Replaying yesterday's scenes
We broke every promise
And spilled all our dreams

A sinner needs to sin
Going back again and again
Who got more than they wanted
Who wanted more than they got

The wars of scars
We don't mean for it to happen
It just happens
When the past won't stay past

Don't let them see the pain
Or they'll be back for more
The brink of madness
Laughs and enjoys the show

The Beast

In a wisp of smoke down on the corner
There was this cat named Fortunate Lee
Talking at me from voices in his head
Yelling about what storyteller said

You've got to be careful here child
There's a beast in the promised land
There's madness you don't understand
The beast is crazed and running wild

Littleboyman littlegirlwoman no big deal
Nothing personal your mind's another meal
Savoring the rush of you like heady wine
Feeding is what the beast is meant to do
Strange are those walls built to hide
Stranger to look and learn not to see
He's in the mask you put on your face
Thought's his favorite breeding place
In the race to midnight it's after eleven
The nature of the beast is all he knows
Behind doors of hell are gates of heaven
Doors are open but the gates are closed

Like trying to break a nasty habit
Me and the beast keep going at it
Some questions helping defend my brain
Serious stuff about serious stuff

Yeah I love you lady and I can't stay
Crazy as I've been is crazy as I am
Want you baby but I can't be your man
Can't bring myself to do us that way

In a wisp of smoke down on the corner
There's this cat named Fortunate Lee
Keeps yelling at me about the beast
And being like the jailhouse dog

My Fire

After every thought is thought
After all is said and done
If you don't like my smoke
Then stay away from my fire

I'm not asking anyone for
Permission to be me, so
Don't be asking questions
That I have to answer
I'm not in control, and
I never will be, so
The realest I can do
Is to influence my part
In my need to be alive
That addiction to live
Before and when there
Was no one to hold me

Think what you want to think
Do what you have to do
Say what you need to say
I'm not listening anyway

A little mistake here
A little mistake there
The reflecting reality
Of nobody's perfect
Nobody's perfect
The happys and the miseries
Do their circling dance
The forgiving and the forgiven
Do they really stand a chance
When nothing turns out right
Well if nothing is right
It must mean nothing is wrong
Now what could that mean

After every thought is thought
After all is said and done
If you don't like my smoke
Then stay away from my fire

Cry Your Tears

Now you want us
To cry your tears for you
After we've already bled for you
Already been dead to you
Now you want us
To cry your tears for you

Chapters of a democracy story
Descendents of genocide
Twelve score and more years ago
We went from being the majority
To being the smallest minority
Now you want us
To cry your tears for you

We saw that emptying
Early morning skyline
Back through that horizon
Duck Valley 1979, Wounded Knee
Sand Creek, that Trail of Tears
Exactly how did our land
Become your country
Now you want us
To cry your tears for you
While we're still crying tears of our own

With your past as your future
That industrial ruling class
Using religion as a weapon
Distilling love into hate
Pointing fingers and name calling evil
Sacrificing lives and blood
Making the innocent the new virgins
Offering to the gods of profit
Now you want us
To cry your tears for you

In the homeland security
Pretending corporate corruption
Isn't economic terrorism
Money talks while the government listens
Compiling files on ones who think different
Conditioning an acceptance of debt
And not to expect the truth
So get used to hearing the lie
Now you want us
To cry your tears for you

Misusing the beauty
Turning freedom into a killing machine
Mass murdering the environment
Weaponizing the psychology of fear
And pushing material addiction with
A substitution of rules faking the law
The bill of rights becomes collateral damage
Making the constitution another broken treaty
Now you want us
To cry your tears for you

Way this story is unfolding
We may end up crying together
As in crying at the same time
But we're short on tears to cry for you
With all these tears to cry of our own
Now you want us
To cry your tears for you

With Yesses

In the melting of molten
This smother of tender
Embracing the tigress
To caress you with yesses

I never believed in heaven
Then you put your arms around me
When you pulled me into you
I knew how happy, happy can be

The memory of all that's good
Riding these rapids of thought
Into the solace of the sun
And ancient pull of the moon

A gathering of blessings
This brighting of life
In the romancing of hearts
This surrounding of clean

Our merging of moment
Take it to the point of love
Embracing the tigress
To caress you with yesses

Our merging of moment
Take it to the point of love
A mating of magic and reality
High flying beyond the stars

I wasn't lost I wasn't found
Now I'm where I'm meant to be
Embracing the tigress
To caress you with yesses

Iktomi

I flew with the eagles
Until I fell from the nest
I ran with the wolves
Then got lost from the pack

Slowly I go crazy every day
Some days run faster than others
I never strayed into heaven
It was hard getting past hell
I traveled through and beyond
The death and birth of man
I am Iktomi

Imagine running out of imagine
Mistaking authority for power
Weaving lifes free spirit
Into patterns of control

I heard all that was said
Until now I hear nothing at all
The edge between twilight and dark
The great lie lurks
Prostitution of soul
Anyone can do it or not
I went down some roads that
Stopped me dead in my tracks
I am Iktomi

I've been the mirror
To others reflecting selves
I've known love that can't help
But love and I've been close
To that hurting way of love

I flew with the eagles
Until I fell from the nest
I ran with the wolves
Then got lost from the pack

From the earth
Wind cave memories
One with the sky
Time of different motions
Dog days dreamer
Chasing the neon
Woven into minds
I am Iktomi

From my place in line
I fell out of order
I've been here
I've been there
I've been anywhere
And
I haven't been anywhere
And I'll be back again
I am Iktomi

Imagine running out of imagine
Mistaking authority for power
Weaving lifes free spirit
Into patterns of control

Make a Chant

Shaman gonna make a chant
A chant a chant
Healing in a song a song a song
Shaman gonna make a chant
A chant a chant
See who you are you are you are

Shaman gonna make a chant
A chant a chant
Listen to your heart your heart your heart
Shaman gonna make a chant
A chant a chant
Share love to care to care to care

Shaman gonna make a chant
A chant a chant
Natural to be free be free be free
Shaman gonna make a chant
A chant a chant
Always do your best your best your best

Peace   word thought consciousness
Only way to live
Peace   man woman brother sister
Remember caring love
Peace   people leading kind lives
Leaders aren't leaders people are
Peace   embrace obligations to truth
Give each generation strong hoops

Peace   our relations all of life
Harmony in all living things
Peace   proclamation not enough
Our responsibility emancipate earth
Peace   our balance channel our flow
Determination in human energy

Peace   past is current to future
We are stronger than we appear
Peace   warmaker so far out of balance
They can't help but fall
Peace   we come from the beginning
A world with no end   life

Shaman gonna make a chant
A chant a chant
Kindness a good word
Good word good word
Shaman gonna make a chant
A chant a chant
Open up your mind
Your mind your mind

Shaman gonna make a chant
A chant a chant
Brothers sisters will unite
Unite unite
Shaman gonna make a chant
A chant a chant
Harmony on earth
On earth on earth

Shaman gonna make a chant
A chant a chant
Peace no war no war no war
Shaman gonna make a chant

Baby Boom Che

You wanna know what happened to Elvis
I'll tell you what happened
I oughta know man I was one of his army
I mean man I was on his side
He made us feel all right
We were the first wave in the
Postwar baby boom

The generation before had just come
Out of the Great Depression and World War II
You know heavy vibes for people to wear
So much heaviness like some kind of
Voiding of the emotions

Their music you know the songs
Life always carries
You know every culture has songs
Well anyway their music was
Restrained emotion
You know like you didn't wanna dance
If you didn't know how
Which says something strange
Well anyway Elvis came along
About ten years after the nuke
When the only generals America had in
The only army she had were Ike and Mac
And stupor hung over the land
A plague where everyone tried to
Materially free themselves
Still too shell-shocked to understand
To feel what was happening

Everything was getting hopeless
Then when Elvis started to rock
The roll just picked up
I mean drabness the beaver showed us
Could only be a foretold future
Who wanted to be Ward and June and
I mean father never did know best
He was still crazy from surviving the war

Like there was this psychotic pall
So widespread as to be assumed normal
Heavy man   you know really
Anyway Elvis showed us an out
You know he showed everyboyman and
Everygirlwoman there's something good
In feeling good
Like a prophet for everyboy everygirl
When someones mom and dad lied
Something about him told us
To be sensual is really okay
Someones mom and dad waltzed us around
Everygirl wasn't supposed to enjoy it
If she did she was bad and everyboy
Well boys will be boys don't feel anything
Take what you can
Marry a decent girl when the fun's done
Like no matter what we did we all were guilty
Maybe someones mom and dad resented
What they missed and while
They were trying to pass it on us
We heard Elvis's song and
For the first time we made up our own mind

The first wave rebelled
I mean we danced even if we didn't know how
I mean Elvis made us move
Instead of standing mute he raised our voice
And when we heard ourselves   something
Was changing you know like for the first time
We made a collective decision about choices

America hurriedly made Pat Boone
A general in the army they wanted us to join
But most of us held fast to Elvis
And the commandants around him
Chuck Berry Buddy Holly Little Richard
Bo Diddley Gene Vincent   you know
Like a different civil war all over again

I mean you take don't be cruel
I want you I need you I love you
And jailhouse rock
Or you take Pat and his white bucks
Singing love letters in the sand
Hell man what's real here
I mean Pat at the beach in his white bucks
His ears getting sunburned told us
Something about old wave delusion
I mean wanting and needing and imprisonment
We all been to those places but what did
White bucks at the beach understand
Other than more straight line dancing
You know what I mean

Anyway man for a while we had a breather
Fresh energy to keep us from falling into the big sleep
Then before long Elvis got assassinated in all the fame
Taking a long time to die   others seized
Control while Elvis rode the needle out
Never understanding what he'd done

It's like we were the baby boom because
Life needed a fresher start
I mean two world wars in a row is
Really crazy man
And Elvis even though he didn't know he said it
He showed it to us anyway and even though
We didn't know we heard it   we heard it anyway

Man like he woke us up
And now they're trying to put us
Back to sleep so we'll see how it goes
Anyway look at the record man
Rock 'n' roll is based on revolution
Going way past 33 1/3
You gotta understand man he was
America's baby boom Che
I oughta know man   I was in his army

Complete Listing of Songs